William Shakespeare

Macbeth

von Horst Mühlmann

Inhaltsangabe der Lektüre als mp3-Download  unter www.klett.de/lernhilfen

Geben Sie den Online-Link 923000-0000 in das Suchfeld links oben ein.

Klett Lerntraining

Dr. Horst Mühlmann, Gymnasiallehrer für Englisch und Deutsch in Bonn, in der Lehrerfortbildung tätig.

Die Akt-, Szenen- und Zeilenangaben zum Dramentext beziehen sich auf die Ausgabe: William Shakespeare, *Macbeth*, edited by Rex Gibson, Cambridge: Cambridge University Press, 2005 (Cambridge School, Shakespeare).

Bibliografische Information der Deutschen Bibliothek
Die Deutsche Bibliothek verzeichnet diese Publikation in der Deutschen Nationalbibliografie; detaillierte bibliografische Daten sind im Internet über http://dnb.ddb.de abrufbar.

Auflage 6. 5. 4. 3. | 2013 2012 2011 2010
Die letzten Zahlen bezeichnen jeweils die Auflage und das Jahr des Druckes.
Alle Rechte vorbehalten.

© Klett Lerntraining GmbH, Stuttgart 2010
1. Auflage 2007
http://www.klett.de/lernhilfen
Umschlagfoto: Klett-Archiv, Stuttgart
Satz: dtp-Studio Andrea Eckhardt, Göppingen
Druck: Beltz Druckpartner, Hemsbach
Printed in Germany
ISBN 978-3-12-923038-1

9 783129 230381

Contents

Preface

Shakespeare's *Tragedy of Macbeth* written in 1606 was probably first performed at Hampton Court in front of King James I and his guest, King Christian IV of Denmark, by Shakespeare's players' company "The King's Men". A performance in Shakespeare's Globe Theatre in 1611 is documented and since then it has been one of the most successful plays on stage all over the world and is also read and even performed at universities and schools. It has not only been adapted to different cultures but also to operas, musicals, films and has been turned into stories, essays, caricatures and satires.

In order to understand the play and its success, it is helpful to know something about the author's life and career as a dramatist and about the period of time he lived in. Therefore the first chapter of this book refers to the sociopolitical, religious and cultural influences on the author, while in the following chapters the play itself is analysed and interpreted. After that, some of its adaptations are described and discussed.

Finally you can work on some tasks which help you to analyse various aspects of the play and to comment on some of its essential themes and problems. Moreover, you can write essays and term papers about *Macbeth* adaptations.

I   The Author and his Times, Life, Stage, and Works

1.   Shakespeare and his Times

Six years before Shakespeare was born on April 23rd, 1564, Elizabeth I had become Queen of England. She belonged to the House of Tudor and was daughter to Anne Boleyn, one of the wives of Henry VIII whom he executed. Elizabeth followed her sister Mary, a devout Roman Catholic, who was called the bloody Queen because after her marriage to the Catholic Philip II of Spain in 1554 she mercilessly persecuted the Protestants and ordered the execution of about 300 Protestants. Among them was Archbishop Cranmer, whose English Prayer Book replaced the Catholic missal under Queen Elizabeth, when she formally re-established the Anglican Church in England.

Under Elizabeth I neither Catholics nor Puritans were allowed to practise their religion openly according to their rites. They were not persecuted as long as they went to church on Sundays pretending to behave like Protestants. Jesuit missionaries and Puritan dissenters who openly tried to win people over to their belief were persecuted and also cruelly executed, e.g. cut to pieces alive (cf. Trevelyan, *Shakespeare's England*, pp. 6 f). Ordinary people were reported to the authorities when they were absent at the church service and suspected of sympathising with the Catholic belief, which also happened to Shakespeare's daughter Susanna. Shakespeare's father was believed to be a Papist, because after his death a Catholic Creed was found hidden under the roofing tiles of his house. Only the Protestant religion (the Anglican Church established by Henry VIII) was favoured "and it was identified in the minds of Englishmen with patriotism, with defiance of Spain, with sea-power and Drake's American adventures, with the protection of the life of the Queen from assassins" (Trevelyan, *A Shortened History of England*, p. 267). Thus the religious problems of the country were not solved by Queen Elizabeth's superficial compromise but led to future conflicts.

Also in politics no opposition was allowed: "no one might criticize the government. Even loyal John Stubbs, for writing a pamphlet advising the Queen not to marry the French Prince Alencon, had his right hand cut off by the hangman. Waving the bloody stump he cried from the scaffold 'Long live the Queen!' Such was the relation of that strange, subtle woman to her simple-hearted subjects" (Trevelyan, 1960, p. 268).

Queen Elizabeth I

The reign of Elizabeth is also called The Golden Age since peace and prosperity spread in the country mainly due to the increase of political and economic power, particularly after the defeat of the Spanish Armada in 1588 by Francis Drake (later knighted by Queen Elizabeth) and his "sea-dogs", all of them pirates and explorers. The economic rise was mainly based on foreign trade, mining and manufacture. Though surely the more privileged classes profited most from the political and economic progress, it was also favourable for craftsmen and traders, artists, writers and players, since "outside the politico-religious sphere, intellectual and poetic freedom had already reached their fullest expansion by the end of Elizabeth's reign" (Trevelyan, 1960, p. 268). Moreover, a Poor Law helped reduce the number of beggars and unemployment.

"Shakespeare and his friends, standing as they did, outside the dangerous world of religious and political controversy, enjoyed in their own spacious domains a freedom of spirit perhaps irrecoverable." (Trevelyan, 1960, p. 269) People of all classes enjoyed life and were fond of dancing, music and sports. They filled the numerous newly built theatres in London and were eager to watch both comic and violent scenes. The theatres had to compete with such cruel entertainment as cockfighting and bear-baiting, which attracted the masses at the Bear-garden near Shakespeare's Globe Theatre on the southern bank of the Thames. That may have been one reason why successful dramatists like Marlowe and Shakespeare also wrote and performed plays full of fighting and blood, cruelty and murder to entertain their audience. Before his final fight Macbeth identifies with a bear fastened to a post by a chain and whipped by its torturer and attacked by fierce dogs (cf. Act 5, Scene 7, lines 1–2).

To get to the Globe or Bear-garden people had to cross the river on London Bridge (see Map, p. 90), the only bridge in those days, with the severed heads of the executed on spikes at the bridge's gates. Even the executions were public entertainment, in particular when even more than twenty delinquents were hanged. Possibly William Shakespeare had also seen his grandfather's head on such a spike after Henry Arden had been executed because he was accused of planning a plot against Queen Elizabeth.

After the victory over the Spanish Armada, England had not only become a world power but Queen Elizabeth also modernised the universities and grammar schools under the influence of the Renaissance, i.e. the rebirth of studies of the classical cultures of ancient Greece and Rome, accompanied by a rising interest in philosophy and science. She read Greek and Latin literature and spoke Italian and French fluently. The universities of Oxford and Cambridge changed from mainly ecclesiastical institutions to places offering secular studies to an increasing number of students including noblemen and poets-to-be such as Sir Philip Sidney, Sir Walter Raleigh, Edmund Spenser and Christopher Marlowe, the most famous and successful dramatist beside Shakespeare in the Elizabethan time.

The standard of the grammar schools was also raised in the Elizabethan time since the teachers had to study in Oxford or Cambridge before getting the job. The grammar schools were open to the most intelligent boys of rich and poor families belonging to the upper and middle classes. It is assumed that as son of an alderman also Shakespeare attended the Grammar School in Stratford. The majority of the people, however, remained illiterates and even Shakespeare's father signed documents by three crosses, as did his wife.

But the Elizabethan period was not only endangered by the threat of the Spanish invasion. It was also haunted by political rivalries, intrigues of the court, plots to murder Elizabeth throughout her reign, religious adversaries, superstition and frequent plagues. Thus the London theatres had to be closed in 1593 because of the "black death" when more than ten thousand people died.

After holding her cousin Mary Stuart of Scotland captive for almost 20 years and hesitating to sign the death warrant, Queen Elizabeth finally agreed to the execution in 1587. Whether Mary Stuart, who had been looking for protection in England after being dethroned in Scotland, had really known of a plot against the Queen had not been proved. After his rebellion against Elizabeth, the Earl of Essex was executed in 1601. Neither Mary Stuart's nor Elizabeth's throne had been really safe. They had to be ready to defend their position and power throughout their reigns, which reminds the reader or spectator of the fates of Shakespeare's kings and queens in his histories and tragedies.

Elizabeth, who is often characterised as strong-willed and her reign supported by her Privy Council and Parliament as strict, is also called the Virgin Queen, since she did not marry and was childless, which was one of the reasons of the fear of political instability after her death. Already one year after her accession to the throne she had declared: "I have already joined myself in marriage to a husband, namely, the Kingdom of England." (Quoted from: Suerbaum, 1989, p. 193)

After her death in 1603, Mary Stuart's son, already James VI of Scotland since 1567, followed her on the throne as James I of England, Scotland and Ireland, alluded to by Shakespeare in *Macbeth* (Act 4, Scene 1, lines 120–121): "And some I see, / That two-fold balls [representing the two orbs James carried at his two coronations in Scotland and England] and treble sceptres [symbolising the three countries] carry." It might be called the irony of fate that the son of Mary Stuart of Scotland, who had been executed under Elizabeth I because of treason, was her successor as James I. He had not protested against his mother's execution in order not to lose his claim to the English throne (cf. Suerbaum, 1989, p. 178). Dramatic and particularly tragic irony is one of the most frequent stylistic devices used by Shakespeare in *Macbeth* and other plays, which is both a means of ridicule and criticism of human follies and vices and man's inconsistent and unpredictable behaviour.

James I was a "good-natured, conceited, garrulous King, wise in book-learning but a poor judge of men, and so ignorant of England and her laws that at Newark he ordered a cut-purse caught in the act to be hanged without trial at a word from his royal mouth." (Trevelyan, 1960, p. 278) He also contributed to the decline of England as a sea-power as he was – contrary to Elizabeth I – not much interested in supporting the navy. When he reinforced the fines for recusancy [i.e. the refusal of Roman Catholics to attend Anglican services as required by law], Guy Fawkes and some other Catholic gentlemen planned the gunpowder plot to kill the King and his ministers at the opening of Parliament. This plot was betrayed on the 5th of November 1605, a date still celebrated as Guy Fawkes Day. The leitmotif of *Macbeth*, equivocation, probably also refers to the Jesuit Henry Garnet (cf. Act 2, Scene 3, lines 7 ff), who defended the right to equivocate, i.e. mislead the court of justice without actually lying, when he was accused of being involved in the gunpowder plot and finally executed.

In 1606, only one year after the Gunpowder Plot, Shakespeare wrote *Macbeth* and possibly refers to the King's escape from the plot in his play (cf. Act 2,

King James I

Scene 3, line 50). But there are obviously more references to King James in *Macbeth* since he appreciated Shakespeare's plays so much that he became the patron of the dramatist's theatre company in 1603, whose name under Queen Elizabeth "The Chamberlain's Men" was changed to "The King's Men". The company was bound by contract to play about twelve performances at court every year. The King probably saw a performance of *Macbeth* in 1606, which seems to have been written for him since in this tragedy Shakespeare deals with Scottish history for the first time. He even changes Banquo's role as Macbeth's accomplice into that of an honest nobleman and loyal subject of King Duncan because Banquo was said to be the source of the royal Stuarts. Moreover, Shakespeare presents the witches as dramatic characters since James I was extremely interested in witchcraft and had his *Daemonologie* re-printed, a book about witchcraft he had written and published in Scotland in 1597. In 1590 the King had also taken part in a trial against a group of "witches", who were accused of trying to murder him. One of them was inter-rogated by the King himself and cruelly tortured. Because of the witch-mania during Elizabeth's and James's reigns hundreds of people were suspected of witchcraft, terribly tortured and burned to death.

Shakespeare was also financially successful because his plays attracted a large audience from all social strata including Queen Elizabeth, James I and their Court. As the population of London grew from about 100,000 people to about 250,000 in the Elizabethan time, the city became the largest town in Europe (beside Paris). It was overcrowded and not only in the poor districts a rather insanitary place, dirty and likely to spread diseases. Several outbreaks of the bubonic plague caused the death of thousands of citizens, which was the reason for the closure of London theatres. But the growth of the population also meant that the numbers of theatres grew according to the rising demand of the citizens for entertainment. Whereas mainly the masses liked to watch battle scenes and murders, and delighted in comic scenes and even crude jokes and a coarse language such as in the Porter Scene of *Macbeth*, the more educated and noble spectators also appreciated the poetic and refined verses of a play and the rhetorically and intellectually demanding elements of the performance.

As the countryside was not far away and four fifths of the four million subjects of Queen Elizabeth lived in the country or in small towns, the audiences in London watching the performances in inn-yards also liked references to nature, which are frequent in Shakespeare's plays since he grew up in a small town, in Stratford-upon-Avon with about 2000 inhabitants, in close relationship with nature. Thus he uses numerous images and comparisons in his works, in *Macbeth* mainly referring to animals that were believed to be evil omens such as hooting owls: "It was the owl that shrieked, the fatal bellman" (Act 2, Scene 2, line 3). In connection with the witches he mentions their cats, venomous reptiles, toads, poisonous plants, etc and refers to bad weather (storm, rain, fog) in contrast to King Duncan's impression of fresh air and summer birds when arriving at Macbeth's castle.

To sum it up, Shakespeare's works can to a certain degree be understood against the background of the period of time he lived in. That applies to the predominant topics of his plays and his language and dramatic style. His works reflect not only his genius but also the status and expectations of his audience as well as the Elizabethan belief in a universal order, the "chain of beings", which "stretched from the foot of God's throne to the meanest of inanimate objects" (Tillyard, 1963, p. 38). At the bottom of this chain were the elements, liquids and metals, followed upwards by the plants, animals, man, the angels and finally God. According to the fundamental belief in monarchy, the plants, animals and men form a monarchy like the colony of bees. For example, the "king" of the stones is the diamond, the "king" of the trees is the oak, the eagle is the king of the birds. Man has to obey the King, who like everybody has to obey God to preserve the world order. But it is also believed that after the Fall of the Angels and of the first men, the divine order is permanently endangered by evil and chaos (cf. Tillyard, 1963, pp. 37 ff, and Suerbaum, 1989, pp. 475 ff). Shakespeare shows this danger in nearly all his plays, also in *Macbeth*, with the evil powers seducing the protagonist and his wife to submit themselves to their destructive influence: "Come, you spirits [...] And fill me from the crown to the toe topfull / Of direst cruelty" (Lady Macbeth, Act 1, Scene 5, lines 38–41); "Come what come may" (Macbeth, Act 1, Scene 3, line 145).

Whereas Macbeth gives up his own will and leaves everything to fate, which in his case means to the evil powers, his comrade Banquo is aware of the danger:

> And oftentimes, to win us to our harm,
> The instruments of darkness tell us truths;
> Win us with honest trifles, to betray's
> In deepest consequence. –
> (Act 1, Scene 3, lines 122–125)

When at the end of the play Macbeth, who is called a "butcher", and his "fiend-like" (devilish) queen are dead (cf. Act 5, Scene 9, line 36), the political and cosmic order has been restored by both the new King of Scotland and the King of England. The restoration of order against disorder, destruction and chaos is Shakespeare's predominant subject in all his histories and tragedies.

2. Shakespeare's Life

As there is no contemporary biography, Shakespeare's life has to be reconstructed based on parish registers, legal documents, pamphlets, business papers, his last will, etc. According to the entry in the parish register of Holy Trinity Church in Stratford-upon-Avon, "Gulielmus filius John Shakespeare" was baptised on April 26th, 1564. As in those days children were usually baptised three days after childbirth, Shakespeare was probably born on April 23rd in his parents' house, a half-timbered building in Henley Street, which is still visited by thousands of visitors from all over the world every year.

His father, John Shakespeare, son of a tenant farmer in Snittersfield near Stratford-upon-Avon, a small town and market place in Warwickshire, went to Stratford and became a successful glover and probably a dealer in leather, wool, and other agricultural products. He advantageously married Mary Arden, one of eight children of Robert Arden, a member of an old-established, prosperous and respected large Catholic family in Warwickshire, who also was the landlord of John Shakespeare's father. John Shakespeare was able to buy houses and plots of land, became an alderman and mayor, and in 1576 applied for a coat of arms for his family and to be recognised as a "Gentleman", which failed because he ran into debts probably because of speculative losses.

Shakespeare's Birthplace

William, the eldest surviving son of eight brothers and sisters of which three died early, probably entered the local Grammar School at the age of seven. School was no bed of roses, since in summer it started at six o'clock, in winter at seven and lasted till the late afternoon for six days a week. On Sundays there was no school but it was obligatory to attend a church service. The teaching language was Latin and apart from translating texts, the predominant teaching method was learning texts by heart and reciting them, e.g. quotations of classical writers which had been collected by Leonhard Culmann in his school book *Sententiae Pueriles*. The pupils read at least parts of the works of Terence, Plautus, Cicero, Sallust, Virgil, and others. Dramatic scenes were also performed. Moreover, the pupils had to translate parts of the Calvinist Bible and learned Greek by having to translate parts of the Greek New Testament. They also learned rhetoric, history and mathematics.

Thus Shakespeare got a solid fundamental education for his career as a player and dramatist. In his works he frequently refers to various classical writers, and apart from the Bible he uses Ovid's *Metamorphoses* – very popular school reading – as his favourite source of images, quotations and allusions showing his extensive literary knowledge. The statement of Shakespeare's rival dramatist and friend Ben Jonson that he only learned "small Latin and less Greek" must not be taken too seriously since it is probably based on Jonson's belief that Shakespeare was less well-read than he himself. It is not known at what age he left school but probably before the ordinary end of school education at 16. It is believed that Shakespeare was educated in the large school-room on the first floor of Stratford's Grammar School, while in the guildhall below he probably saw his first plays performed by travelling companies of actors.

In 1582 Shakespeare married Anne Hathaway, daughter of a wealthy farmer in Shottery near Stratford. She was eight years older than William and already expecting their daughter Susanna, who was born six months later. Their twins Hamnet and Judith were born in 1585. Whereas Hamnet already died at the age of eleven, Susanna married Dr Hall, a wealthy medical doctor in Stratford, and in the year of the playwright's death his daughter Judith married the wine merchant Thomas Quiney, whose three children died young.

There are no documents that could inform us about Shakespeare's life between 1585 and 1592. But it is assumed that Shakespeare went to London some years before 1592 when the playwright Robert Greene already on his death-bed wrote a letter to three of his fellow dramatists, probably Marlowe, Nashe and Peele, warning them of the players who take the credit for what other playwrights, who were educated at universities, have written. In particular he attacks Shakespeare and calls him an upstart who believes himself to be the only dramatist who "shakes" the stage by his plays, i.e. who believes himself to surpass the other dramatists and to be the most popular and successful playwright in London:

> "Yes, trust them not: for there is an upstart crow, beautiful with our feathers, that with his tiger's heart wrapped in a player's hide, supposes he is as well able to bombast out a blank verse as the best of you: and […] is in his own conceit the only Shake-scene in the country." (Quoted from: Suerbaum, 1989, p. 355)

But a few weeks later, Greene's publisher published an apology in which he stressed Shakespeare's honesty and his "facetious grace in writing that approves his art". Six years later, Francis Meres praises Shakespeare and his works in his *Palladis Tamia* ("Treasure of Pallas"), a collection of poetic quotations:

> "As the soul of *Euphorbus* was thought to live in *Pythagoras*: so the sweet witty soul of *Ovid* lives in mellifluous and honey-tongued *Shakespeare*, witness his *Venus and Adonis*, his *Lucrece*, his sugared sonnets among his private friends, etc. As *Plautus* and *Seneca* are accounted the best for comedy and tragedy among the Latins: so *Shakespeare* among the English is the most excellent in both kinds for the stage […]. As *Epius Stolo* said that the muses would speak with *Plautus'* tongue if they would speak Latin: so I say that the muses would speak with *Shakespeare's* fine filed phrase if they would speak English." (Quoted from: Suerbaum, 1989, pp. 363–364)

In 1593 and 1594 Shakespeare published two short epic poems, *Venus and Adonis* and *The Rape of Lucrece*, which he dedicated to Henry Wriothesly, Earl of Southampton, to whom he also dedicated his 154 sonnets, which were probably written between 1594 and 1597 and circulated among his friends before they were published in 1609 without Shakespeare's consent.

As in 1572 Queen Elizabeth had enacted a law which allowed common players to be treated as vagabonds and criminals unless they belonged to a peer, players' companies had to find a patron who protected them as members of his court. Shakespeare probably began his career as a player in a company called Leicester's Men and was already a successful playwright, too, when in 1594 he joined The Lord Chamberlain's Men, named after a high court official who had to grant permission for the performance of a new play. Consequently the best playwrights and players wanted to become members of this company, which played at Queen Elizabeth's Court 32 times and was renamed in The King's Men under James I when he came to the throne in 1603. They performed the tragedy of *Macbeth* among other great plays written by Shakespeare. It is assumed that Shakespeare, who used to play smaller parts in his plays, played the role of King Duncan.

As Shakespeare was extraordinarily successful as a player, playwright and also a sharer (partner) of the Globe Theatre and Blackfriars, he was able to support his family financially and buy houses and land in and around his home town. For his father, his children and children's children he obtained the coat of arms showing a golden spear with a silver tip in 1596, which his father had not been able to afford. Thus also Shakespeare belonged to the gentry and was entitled to call himself "Gentleman".

As he was a prosperous gentleman now, he finished his work for the theatre, left London and spent his last three or four years before his death in his big house New Place in Stratford managing his property. He died on his birthday, April 23rd, 1616 and was buried in the chancel of Holy Trinity Church. The bust of the playwright was erected nearby on the north wall within seven years of his death and in the lifetime of his widow, who was buried alongside his grave in 1623 when his friends and colleagues of The King's Men published the first collection of his plays, the First Folio. The bust and the copperplate engraving of the First Folio are the only "authentic" portraits of Shakespeare in so far as they really show the playwright and were probably produced according to the instructions of the citizens and friends who ordered them and had known the dramatist personally.

Mr. WILLIAM

SHAKESPEARES

COMEDIES,
HISTORIES, &
TRAGEDIES.

Published according to the True Originall Copies.

Martin Droeshout sculpsit London.

LONDON
Printed by Isaac Iaggard, and Ed. Blount. 1623.

First Folio Engraving of Shakespeare

3.   Shakespeare's Theatre

As travelling actors also visited Stratford, Shakespeare probably saw the first plays performed in the guildhall and in inn-yards where the play-wagons usually arrived and attracted the citizens, who were entertained by morality plays (presenting personified virtues and vices), interludes (comic scenes), comedies and tragedies usually written by the players themselves.

When two play-wagons were pushed together, there was a fairly long stage with two scaffolds at each end, whose lower storey was used for "in-door" actions such as in a house or room, whereas on the upper storey scenes on the wall of a castle were played. The players had to climb up the dressing-room underneath the stage and entered or left the stage while the curtains at the lower storey were briefly opened and closed. Throughout the performance the stage and the storeys were open with the curtains withdrawn.

Some of these fundamental elements of that stage and the inn-yard are also characteristic of the Shakespearean theatre and stage. There is the open stage without curtains (possibly a rear stage with curtains for scenes inside a building) and the dressing-room or cellerage underneath the stage with a trapdoor for instance for the appearance and disappearance of ghosts and witches. Whether there were the two scaffolds, too, cannot be proved, since the only picture of an Elizabethan stage drawn by Johannes de Witt, a young Dutch traveller, about 1596 (see p. 18) does not show them but only a large stage protruding into the auditorium so that the performance could be seen from three sides.

The stage itself is not subdivided and scenes could be played in front, at the rear or any other part of the stage, which is covered by a roof on two columns. At the rear there is the property-room for the mostly rich costumes and stage property. The players can leave or enter through two doors. Above there is a gallery for spectators, which might have also be used for scenes on the wall of a castle as in *Macbeth*. On top of the rear building is a turret with a flag to show that there will be a performance, which begins with the signal of a trumpeter.

Around the apron stage were three tiers of galleries usually for the spectators of higher ranks or those who could afford tickets at a higher price, e.g. merchants and young lawyers from the Inns of Court. Courtiers were also allowed to sit on stools at the rear of the stage. Common people, who only paid one penny, which was the price of a loaf of bread, had to stand in the crowded courtyard around the stage and were not protected against rain or sunshine since there was no roof. The so-called "groundlings" were mainly students, workers and apprentices who sometimes also left work to see a play, since the performances began at two o'clock in the afternoon. They were eating, drinking, heckling, applauding or booing and there was a constant coming and going.

The Swan Theatre drawn by Johannes de Witt (about 1596)

As the plays were performed in the afternoon, Shakespeare helped the audience imagine other times such as night-time by mentioning or referring to the moon or night animals, as in *Macbeth* e.g. in Act 2, Scene 1, lines 1–3 when Banquo asks his son: "How goes the night, boy?" and is answered: "The moon is down", or in Act 3, Scene 2, lines 52–53 when Macbeth says: "Good things of day begin to droop and drowse, / Whiles night's black agents to their preys do rouse."

Though the actors tried to perform the plays rather realistically by fencing, dancing and singing on the stage, there were no sets and not much stage property. The audience was supposed to imagine the different places of action when a table or bed was used to suggest a room or a tree symbolised a forest or only one sign indicated the scenery. Sounds such as the noise of battle-scenes, of thunder and lightning were produced by fire-workers and drummers, and could also be referred to in the verses spoken by the characters, as in *Macbeth* (Act 1, Scene 1, lines 1–2) when the first witch asks the questions:

> When shall we three meet again?
> In thunder, lightning or in rain?

Fog and mist could be produced by burning resin, e.g. when the witches disappear chanting the spell:

> Fair is foul, and foul is fair,
> Hover through the fog and filthy air.
>   (Act 1, Scene 1, lines 12–13)

The costumes, however, were – though not necessarily historically authentic – rather costly and splendid.

The playhouses were octagonal or round buildings, without a roof and therefore also called open theatres such as Shakespeare's Globe Theatre for about 2000 spectators, which was built in 1599. Shakespeare himself refers to it as "this wooden O" at the beginning of his history play *The Life of Henry the Fifth* (Prologue, line 13). As the distance between the actors at the front of the stage and the most distant spectator was only about 25 m, the intimacy between players and audience contributed to the success of the performances. Thus soliloquies for instance seemed to be confidentially addressed to the audience.

After Queen Elizabeth's decree, the actors in London had won recognition, since their apprenticeship lasted seven years before they became leading players. They were also highly-trained in fencing, singing and dancing, which the Elizabethans were very fond of and inspired Shakespeare to make ample use of such scenes in his plays. Because of the continuous demand for new plays the actors continually had to learn new roles in a short time without forgetting the old ones. They had to play their parts without much rehearsing and frequently played more than one part.

The best players' companies had a noble patron, belonged to his court and performed plays also at the Royal Court. The nobility wished to be entertained by them whereas the Puritan London town councils criticised the moral decline since boys played the women's parts. As women were not allowed to become actors and the boys were strictly trained from their childhood, the Puritan criticism was based on traditional prejudices, which also included the violation of the divine order when common players performed the roles of kings. Moreover, they believed that the spectators could follow the immoral examples presented in the plays such as murder, rebellion and adultery. The city authorities knew that prostitutes and thieves mingled with the audience and also feared the danger of infection in the crowded theatres due to the bubonic plague. Therefore the theatres were closed in 1593, 1603 and 1608.

Before public playhouses were built, performances had been given in inns. Because of the city authorities' resistance and even prohibition, most of the theatres were built outside the city walls in the north-east of London, such as the first public open-air theatre called "The Theatre". It was built in 1576 by James Burbage, a carpenter who had become a player. When it had to be pulled down because the lease ran out, he built the famous Globe Theatre from the timber of The Theatre for about 2000 spectators outside the city in Southwark in 1599 with Shakespeare as one of his partners, who had a fifth share in its profits. When it burnt to the ground in 1613 because a sound-effect cannon set fire to the thatch, it was rebuilt only a year later.

Though other playhouses were erected in the north-east or north-west of London such as The Curtain (1577), The Fortune (1600) and the Red Bull Theatre, the most important theatres were built on the South Bank of the Thames, in Southwark, which was considered the entertainment district with bear-baiting, pubs and brothels. They were called The Rose (1587), The Swan (1595) and The Hope (1613). Whereas these theatres were roofless, Shakespeare's Blackfriars Theatre had a roof so that performances were possible throughout the year. It was built on the site of a former monastery in the City and therefore could not be controlled by the city authorities. On the whole there were about 20 theatres whose task was to entertain London's citizens from all social strata.

Though mainly Puritan citizens criticised the theatres as immoral, the Royal Court supported them as long as they performed politically correct plays. After having become the patron of her own company of players, Queen Elizabeth's Men, the Queen protected the performances of plays against the opposition of the Puritans. This practice was continued by her successor James I, who became the patron of Shakespeare's company of players, The King's Men. Queen Elizabeth and James I invited the players' companies to the Court for entertainment. Thus Shakespeare's company gave 32 performances at Queen Elizabeth's Court and from her death till 1616 even 177 performances at King James's Court.

4.   Shakespeare's Plays

When in 1592 the playwright Robert Greene criticised Shakespeare as an "up-start crow", he was driven by envy of Shakespeare's success of his first plays such as the three parts of *Henry VI*. Greene's bitterness is comprehensible because, contrary to the players, playwrights were not really able to become financially successful since they sold their play to a players' company for a modest sum of money and had to write a new play if they wanted to survive. Shakespeare, however, earned money as a player, a playwright and joint owner of two playhouses. He wrote two plays a year on average till after his splendid career he left London for Stratford where he was the second richest citizen.

Usually the playwrights could not earn money by publishing their plays because there was no copyright and the plays could be written down during the performance by a bookseller's clerk and sold afterwards as faulty as they were. So some of Shakespeare's plays were published as unauthorized quarto editions. A collection of 36 comedies, histories and tragedies, which Shakespeare had written between 1590 and 1612, was published by his fellow-actors John Heminge and Henry Condell in 1623 as the First Folio Edition with an engraving of the playwright on the title page (see p. 16) and the list of the principal players with Shakespeare at its head followed by one of the most famous players of Shakespeare's company, Richard Burbage, the son of James Burbage, the builder and owner of The Globe.

The play *Troilus and Cressida* is added in writing to the table of contents, probably because it was difficult for the editors to decide whether this play really is a tragedy instead of a comedy. The romance or comedy *Pericles* and the comedy *The Two Noble Kinsmen*, which was probably written in cooperation with the dramatist John Fletcher, are not included in the First Folio.

In the First Folio, 36 of Shakespeare's 38 plays are categorised as comedies, histories or tragedies. But as these genres are not strictly defined in Shakespeare's time, there is no clear dividing line between the tragedies and the histories, which because of the predominant topic of the rise and fall of kings could also be called tragedies. Francis Meres for example enumerates some plays of Shakespeare in his *Palladis Tamia* (1598) and calls several histories such as *Richard III* tragedies and also *The Merchant of Venice*, which is categorised as a comedy in the First Folio.

Tragedies also contain comic scenes such as the Porter Scene in *Macbeth*. Some of the comedies such as *The Winter's Tale* differ from other Shakespearean comedies to such an extent that they are called romances, which are rather tragicomedies. The following table, which has been slightly adapted (cf. Browning/Arndt, pp. VIII f), may inform you about the main phases of Shakespeare's development as a playwright. It offers an approximate chronology since the exact dates and order of the plays are unknown. But the table might also encourage you to read one play or another apart from *Mac-*

beth or go to the theatre to see the performance of a play you are interested in or watch a film adaptation of one of the plays.

(1) The period of dramatic apprenticeship (1590 – 94)		
Histories	**Comedies**	**Tragedies**
Henry VI (Part I, II, III) Richard III Richard II	Love's Labour's Lost The Two Gentlemen of Verona The Comedy of Errors The Taming of the Shrew	Titus Andronicus
(2) The period of deeper insight in realities and characters (1595 – 99)		
Histories	**Comedies**	**Tragedies**
King John Henry IV (Parts I and II) Henry V	A Midsummer Night's Dream The Merchant of Venice Much Ado About Nothing The Merry Wives of Windsor As You Like It	Romeo and Juliet Julius Caesar
(3) The period of maturity (1600 – 09): Gloomy seriousness, even in the comedies		
	Comedies	**Tragedies**
	Twelfth Night or What You Will All's Well that Ends Well Measure for Measure	Hamlet Troilus and Cressida Othello King Lear Macbeth Timon of Athens Antony and Cleopatra Coriolanus
(4) The period of Romances (1610 – 13): Regal serenity and gentleness of mood		
History		**Romances/Tragicomedies**
Henry VIII (1613)		Pericles Cymbeline The Winter's Tale The Tempest The Two Noble Kinsmen

Shakespeare's success was based on his talent to entertain an audience from all social strata by dealing with various topics and making use of a great variety of language and style. Thus he continues the traditionally popular tragedies of revenge with *Titus Andronicus* (1590), which even surpasses the horror and atrocities of Kyd's *Spanish Tragedy* (1589). Christopher Marlowe (1564 – 93) was the most successful Elizabethan playwright and representative of the New Drama before Shakespeare, and his plays such as *Tamburlaine the Great* and *Doctor Faustus* mainly deal with the lust for power, which Shakespeare also focuses on in many of his plays, e. g. in *Richard III* and *Macbeth*.

The so-called New Drama was influenced by the Interludes, one-act plays of representatives of well-known professions (types), which had developed from the comic scenes of the medieval morality plays presenting the fight of personified Vices and Virtues for man's soul. But the New Drama was particularly based on the classical plays by Seneca or Plautus, which Shakespeare had probably read at school and which were published in English in the 16th century. The playwrights exploited those sources rather extensively and Shakespeare also made use of them and of other sources such as Plutarch's *Lives* and the second edition of Raphael Holinshed's *The Chronicles of England, Scotlande, and Irelande* (1587), which he also used for *Macbeth*, though he changed the plot and the characters according to the expectations of his audience and in particular to flatter James I, at whose court the play was probably performed for the first time.

But as Shakespeare replaces the types and personified passions of former plays by individual characters whose inner conflicts become essential elements of the plot in his histories, comedies, tragedies and romances, his plays surpass the plays of his fellow-dramatists. That may be also a reason why his plays even today fascinate directors, players and spectators and are the most frequently performed and also adapted plays all over the world. Shakespeare's fellow-dramatist Ben Jonson seems to be right when he stated, after his friend's death: "He was not of an age but for all time."

To Shakespeare the world is a stage and man is a player of many roles:

> All the world is a stage,
> And all the men and women merely players;
> They have their exits and their entrances,
> And one man in his time plays many parts.
> (*As You Like It*, Act 2, Scene 7, lines 139–142)

Macbeth's tragic part is to finally realise the absurdity of his life:

> Life's but a walking shadow, a poor player
> That struts and frets his hour upon the stage
> And then is heard no more.
> (Act 5, Scene 5, lines 23–25)

These quotations may represent the wide range of Shakespeare's plays between the joy of living and despair. And when Shakespeare's theatre is called The Globe and the motto is "Totus mundus agit histrionem" ("all the world performs plays"), he claims that the theatre is able to depict the world on a small scale, since the Creator has constructed the world as a great theatre (cf. Suerbaum, 1989, p. 443). In the Renaissance, the idea of the world as a stage was common in Europe and for instance used by Calderon (1600–81) as the title of his play *El gran teatro del mundo* ("The World's Great Stage").

II *The Tragedy of Macbeth*

www.klett.de

1. Contents and Commentary

Act 1, Scene 1

Macbeth does not begin with a scene in which the protagonist of the play is introduced to the audience but with a thunderstorm and the appearance of three witches. They meet on a deserted field and agree on meeting again on the heath before sunset when the battle is over. There they wish to meet Macbeth. They disappear to return to their familiars, i.e. evil demons in the form of animals, a grey cat and a toad, while chanting the paradoxical and ambiguous spell "Fair is foul, and foul is fair". On the Shakespearean stage the witches appear and disappear in mist or fog and filthy air, which was produced by burning resin so that the players were shrouded in smoke and left the stage through a trapdoor.

As in the Elizabethan time it was commonly believed that witches sold their souls to the devil in order to obtain their magic powers, Shakespeare creates an atmosphere of evil at the very beginning of the play, which is characteristic of most of the following scenes. By their magic spell at the end of this very short scene the witches express their main intention, namely to mingle good and evil and thus make it difficult or even impossible for man to distinguish between what is bad and what is good.

Scene 2

Also in the second scene of Act 1 the protagonist does not yet appear on the stage but King Duncan of Scotland, his two sons Malcolm and Donaldbain, a thane (chieftain) and some followers. In Duncan's military camp near Forres they listen to "a bleeding Captain's" (officer's) report about the offstage battle against the rebels. The severely wounded officer, who saved Malcolm from being taken prisoner, praises Macbeth's courage and describes how relentlessly he killed the rebels' leader Macdonald. Together with Banquo, Macbeth went on fighting fearlessly when they had to face fresh Norwegian troops that had invaded Scotland to support the rebellion.

The Thane of Ross arrives and reports that the traitor Cawdor has been captured and the battle, which was already mentioned by the witches, has been won. Duncan orders the execution of the Thane of Cawdor and confers his title on Macbeth.

The wounded officer confronts the audience with the theme of violence and blood, which is predominant throughout the play. Macbeth is indirectly introduced to the audience as a courageous and cruel fighter, who ferociously slices Macdonald from the navel to the jaws. As he rescues the King and Scotland, his honour and loyalty are not questioned.

King Duncan is introduced as a just, gracious and compassionate monarch since he cares for the wounded captain, punishes the traitor and rewards Macbeth for the victory over the rebels and the Thane of Cawdor with the traitor's title. But Duncan is also characterised as a guileless and a too confiding person because he trusts Macbeth without thinking of the possibility that also Macbeth might become a traitor or even his murderer, which Shakespeare seems to foreshadow by the means of dramatic irony: When at the end of this scene Duncan refers to Macbeth's new title by saying: "What he hath lost, noble Macbeth hath won," he uses nearly the same words as the witches when they said that the battle was not yet lost or won. Thus Shakespeare also seems to allude to the mysterious influence of the witches on the King, which Duncan is not aware of.

Scene 3

As arranged in the first scene of the play, the three witches meet on the heath at sunset and tell each other about their evil deeds and plans. One of them returns from killing pigs, probably through swine fever as was believed in Shakespeare's time. Another witch intends to damage a sailor's ship in a heavy storm because his wife did not give her a chestnut and called her a dirty old woman, which underlines the discrepancy between the trivial cause of her revenge and the evil deed. As the first witch wants to make it impossible for the sailor to sleep, Shakespeare also anticipates Macbeth's fear of not being able to sleep any more after Duncan's murder.

Before Macbeth and Banquo enter the stage for the first time, the witches announce Macbeth's arrival by the onomatopoeic couplet "A drum, a drum; / Macbeth doth come" (lines 28–29) and then chant a spell. Macbeth's very first words "So foul and fair a day I have not seen" (line 36) refer to the weather but as they are nearly the same as the witches' words in their spell at the beginning of the play, Shakespeare also ironically alludes to the witches' mysterious influence on Macbeth, though he is not aware of it yet.

When the witches see the two thanes who ask them who they are, they instead of replying greet Macbeth by his present title of Thane of Glamis, then as Thane of Cawdor and finally as the future King. Macbeth winces as if caught thinking about becoming king and Banquo realises that Macbeth is spellbound and confused by the witches' words and seems to "fear / Things that do sound so fair" (lines 49–50). When Banquo asks the witches to tell his future, they prophesy that his descendants will be kings. Macbeth wants them to tell him from where they have their knowledge, but the witches do not answer and disappear.

The Thanes of Ross and Angus arrive and tell Macbeth that King Duncan out of gratitude for Macbeth's victory has bestowed on him the title of Thane of Cawdor, who will be executed for high treason. Whereas the audience already knows that Duncan has decided to confer this honour on Macbeth, Macbeth is completely surprised and believes that the witches' prophecy has come true. Banquo spontaneously asks himself if the witches as instruments of the devil can tell the truth: "What, can the devil speak true?" (line 105). But in fact it was no prophecy: the evil spirits had merely got to know Duncan's decision in a mysterious way before they met Macbeth, who, however, believes the witches and thinks that also their third prediction might come true. Though Banquo assumes that Macbeth might desire to become king now, he contrary to Macbeth is aware of the possibility that the witches try to seduce them by telling evident facts in order to ruin them in the end:

> And oftentimes, to win us to our harm,
> The instruments of darkness tell us truths;
> Win us with honest trifles, to betray's
> In deepest consequence.
>
> (Act 1, Sene 3, lines 122 ff)

The spectators possibly also doubt that the witches' prophecies can automatically come true since the power of the witches is limited. For instance in the first scene of the play they have to admit that they are not able to kill the sailor but only send storms that do damage to his ship. Similarly they are not able to really prophesy Duncan's murder but can only seduce Macbeth to decide to kill the King despite his terribly bad conscience.

In his soliloquy, Macbeth states that the "two truths" (his title of Thane of Glamis, which he inherited from his father Sinel, and the title of Thane of Cawdor) might prove that his becoming king will also come true. But contrary to Banquo he does not presume that the witches might betray him, but reflects on the implications of the predictions, which "cannot be ill, cannot be good" (line 130). On the one hand the witches told him the "truth", i.e. evident facts. But on the other hand their third prophecy does not mean that Macbeth is determined to kill Duncan since he is appalled at the thought of murdering the King who in Shakespeare's time was believed to be the representative of God on earth and whose task it was to defend God's order against evil. Instead of following his moral doubts, he for the moment decides to accept his "fate" and stay passive. By his passiveness, however, he enables the evil spirits to influence him and later on also his wife to urge him to murder Duncan against his scruples and despite his guilty conscience.

Before they leave to meet King Duncan, Macbeth is not honest with Banquo when he tells him that he is thinking about "things forgotten". Also his suggestion that later on they should talk about the witches' words frankly cannot be taken seriously. Thus Shakespeare makes the audience aware of Macbeth's deceitful behaviour, which is even strengthened by Lady Macbeth in the following scenes.

Scene 4

At the Royal Palace at Forres, Malcolm informs King Duncan about the execution of Cawdor. Though he was a traitor, Cawdor is characterised as a courageous and repentant man who confessed his treason and asked for the King's forgiveness before he died. Thus Cawdor is just the opposite of the traitor and murderer Macbeth at the end of the play, who desperately fights against Macduff without any hope or remorse. Duncan admits that he trusted Cawdor absolutely and recognises that it is impossible to read a man's thoughts in his face. Nevertheless he trusts Macbeth now without the slightest idea that the new Thane of Cawdor might become another traitor. Duncan expresses his deeply felt gratitude to Macbeth and Banquo and promises to reward them. Macbeth stresses his loyalty to the king and his duty to serve him, which "pays itself".

After having announced that his son Malcolm shall become Prince of Cumberland and be his successor to the throne, Duncan also honours Macbeth by wishing to be Macbeth's guest at his castle in Inverness. Macbeth wants to be the messenger who informs his wife about the King's arrival. But in an aside Macbeth expresses his ambition to become king and that Malcolm is in his way. He even asks the stars not to shine at night and thus hide his evil desires. As the new King of Scotland was elected by the thanes and not nominated by the King, Duncan makes the mistake of appointing his son as his successor and thus denies Macbeth's rights to the throne, who as Duncan's cousin could also be elected King of Scotland after Duncan's death.

Night is often used as an image of crime and death in this play, and many of the following scenes take place at night. But as the play was performed in broad daylight, much of its setting was left to the audience's imagination.

Scene 5

At Inverness castle, Lady Macbeth reads her husband's letter, in which he describes his meeting with the witches and informs her about their "prophecies". He also alludes to her becoming queen and asks her to keep it a secret. She is at once determined to plan Duncan's murder. As she believes that her husband is ambitious but not able and willing to kill Duncan, she decides to do her utmost to persuade him since fate and the supernatural powers have intended him to become king. She knows her husband's character and is aware of her necessary role to urge him to become a murderer.

When an attendant tells her that Duncan is going to arrive, she first seems to be startled but then invokes the evil spirits to take all kind and tender feelings from her heart and make her extremely cruel and merciless. She does not at all doubt whether the murder should be committed or not but wishes that the murderous deed will be hidden by the devil and not be prevented by God. In Shakespeare's times the audience understood her behaviour literally, i.e. the evil spirits really took possession of Lady Macbeth as if she became a witch, too.

When Macbeth arrives, she welcomes him by greeting him nearly in the same way as the witches in Scene 3: "Great Glamis, worthy Cawdor, / Greater than both by the all-hail hereafter" (lines 52–53). Similar to the mysterious relationship between the witches and Macbeth, Shakespeare also alludes to the witches' influence on Lady Macbeth. Contrary to his wife, Macbeth addresses her with "My dearest love" (line 56) to underline their personal and emotional relationship.

In order to hide their true intentions, she asks him to look innocent when Duncan arrives and as she knows that her husband is doubtful about the murder, she wants him to leave everything to her. As the spectators already know that Duncan is guileless, they expect that Macbeth and his wife will successfully deceive him.

Scene 6

When Duncan and his followers approach Macbeth's castle, the King and Banquo praise the beautiful place and the mild weather. In contrast to Lady Macbeth's words before, Duncan praises the love and kindness of his hostess and asks God to reward her for the trouble of his visit. Thus Shakespeare again uses an ambiguous and ironical style to stress the difference between what people say and what is going to happen. Lady Macbeth welcomes the King with great courtesy and feigns friendliness and gratitude. She even hypocritically tells him that she and her husband constantly pray for him.

At the end of the scene, Duncan wants to see Macbeth and repeats that he has decided to reward him by saying "we love him highly" (line 30), which again stresses the discrepancy between the King's kind feelings and Macbeth's murderous inclination. With the polite phrase "By your leave, hostess" (line 32) Duncan leaves the stage and does not appear again since he will be murdered offstage in the following Act.

Scene 7

While Duncan is being honoured by a banquet offstage, Macbeth wishes to murder the King as soon as possible but without its consequences. In a monologue he utters his fear of vengeance and damnation since Duncan is a virtuous king and absolutely trusts him. Macbeth knows that there is no reason to commit the crime since Duncan relies on him as his cousin, his loyal subject and his host whose duty it is to protect his guest. Moreover, Duncan is a just and gentle king whose murder would mean eternal damnation to the murderer. The only motive left for Macbeth is his restless ambition, which he fears might lead to his downfall.

When his wife interrupts his doubtful reflections, he tells her that he has decided not to kill the King. But Lady Macbeth appeals to his love for her, which also depends on his being "a man" and not a coward. She finishes her urging Macbeth to murder the King by characterising herself as a horrifyingly inhuman mother who would even cruelly kill her baby if she had sworn to do it. As Macbeth fears that they might fail, his wife assures him that her murderous plan cannot fail, because she intends to make the King's body-guards drunk, besmear them with the King's blood and put the blood-stained daggers beside them so that they will be believed to be Duncan's murderers. Macbeth and his wife intend to look innocent and after the murder they want to deceive everybody by feigning horror and grief. Lady Macbeth has finally persuaded her husband to murder the King; Macbeth is now resolved to commit the horrible crime.

Act 2, Scene 1

At night Banquo and his son Fleance meet Macbeth in the courtyard of his castle. While Banquo is disarming before going to bed, he tells Macbeth that Duncan is sleeping. He gives Macbeth a ring, the King's present for Lady Macbeth's hospitality. Whereas Banquo is haunted by his dream about the three witches and their "prophecies", Macbeth pretends not to think of them but then proposes to talk about that matter at another time. Banquo consents but expresses that he will never become unfaithful to the King. Apparently Macbeth and Banquo have become suspicious of each other.

When Macbeth is alone he has the hallucination of a blood-stained dagger which magically seems to urge him to kill Duncan. His mind is filled with images of Hecate's evil activities at night and he asks the earth to silence his steps when he walks to Duncan's room. As Duncan is a good king, Macbeth's last words before the murder are inappropriate if they refer to the King only. They ironically apply both to the victim ("heaven") and to the murderer ("hell").

Scene 2

Shakespeare does not show Duncan's murder on stage, possibly out of consideration for his patron King James I, since Duncan was a gracious and pious king and King James was surely more interested in the final defeat of the King's murderer than to watch the murder of one of his predecessors. Another reason why the murder is committed offstage may be that Shakespeare does not want to create an external atmosphere of suspense by presenting a cruel murder to the audience but wants to focus the audience's attention on the interior process, i.e. Lady Macbeth's and her husband's reaction to the crime.

The scene is introduced by Lady Macbeth waiting for her husband's return after the murder and reflecting on having put a harmful drug into the drinks of Duncan's servants while she is listening intently and hearing an owl that she calls "the fatal bellman" (the watchman who rang the bell before executions and burials). She fears that her husband has not killed Duncan even though she has laid the bodyguards' daggers ready for him.

As she needed alcohol to make her "bold" and admits that she would not have been able to kill the King because he resembled her father, the audience learns that she is not as cruel and relentless as she pretends to be, which seems to foreshadow her helplessness at the end of the play.

Macbeth appears with two blood-stained daggers and blood on his hands. He expresses his horror by shouting short questions and asks his wife if she has heard a noise, which she denies. But referring to Macbeth's short questions she asks him in return whether the voice he heard was not his own voice. By the following fast exchange of short questions and replies, frequently only one-word sentences (stichomythia) between the couple (lines 16 ff) Shakespeare emphasises the tension:

> LADY MACBETH Did not you speak?
> MACBETH When?
> LADY MACBETH Now.
> MACBETH As I descended?
> LADY MACBETH Ay.

Macbeth is horrified when he looks at his hands: "This is a sorry sight" (line 23) while his wife repeats his words saying: "A foolish thought, to say a sorry sight" (line 24) by which Shakespeare also alludes to her madness at the end of the play. Though Macbeth does not describe the murder itself, he depicts what he saw and heard in that moment. He is extremely shocked by the fact that he could not say "Amen" when Duncan's attendants said their prayers because he "had most need of blessing" (line 35). He is horrified by the idea that he will never be able to sleep again since he believes that by murdering the sleeping King he has "murdered sleep" (line 45) itself.

Lady Macbeth tries to calm him down by admonishing him not "to think / So brain-sickly of things" (lines 48–49) but wash his hands. She also warns him that such thoughts will "make us mad" (line 37). Thus Shakespeare alludes again to her mental breakdown at the end of the play when she is sleepwalking and trying to wash the imaginary blood off her hands.

Macbeth has brought the daggers of the sleeping bodyguards and is shocked by his deed to such an extent that he does not dare to return and leave them beside the sleeping men:

> I'll go no more
> I am afraid to think what I have done;
> Look on't again, I dare not.
>
> (Act 2, Sene 2, lines 53–55)

Lady Macbeth, however, blames her husband's childish fear and leaves to besmear the bodyguards with Duncan's blood. When she comes back with blood-stained hands she pretends to be ashamed "to wear a heart so white" (line 68), i.e. that she did not commit the murder herself.

Whereas Macbeth's horror of his bloody "hangman's hands" (line 30) is stressed by his fear that the blood will rather turn the oceans red than be cleaned (cf. lines 63 ff), Lady Macbeth plays everything down when she returns with blood-stained hands by saying: "A little water clears us of this deed" (line 70).

When they hear a knock at the castle's gate several times, Macbeth is appalled by it whereas Lady Macbeth decides that they should retreat to their sleeping-room and wash their hands to have an alibi. Macbeth, however, cannot understand why he was able to kill Duncan and wishes that he had not murdered him but that the knocking would wake the King:

> To know my deed, 'twere best not know my self.
> Wake Duncan with thy knocking: I would thou couldst.
> (Act 2, Scene 2, lines 76–77)

Scene 3

The knocking continues and wakes up the drunken porter of the castle, who imagines himself to be the porter of Hell and asks himself several questions that refer to the devil and his opening the gate of Hell for a greedy farmer, a liar and a fraudulent tailor.

Shakespeare seems to interrupt the murderous action by "comic relief", which is meant to lighten the extreme tension of the action for a while but also to heighten the horror of the previous and the following scene. As the porter enumerates several human vices and reminds the audience of eternal damnation, he is both comic and to be taken seriously when he not only addresses the newcomers, Macduff and Lennox, but also the audience: "I pray you, remember the porter" (lines 16–17). Macbeth's porter is in fact a porter of "Hell" since Macbeth's castle is the place of Macbeth's crime and damnation. Moreover, he is well-known by the audience as a character of the morality plays, i.e. the Porter of Hell's Gate, who admits sinners to hell. Thus Shakespeare also hints at Macbeth's and his wife's eternal damnation and reminds the audience of the day of doom.

Shakespeare continues using this ambiguous and rude style in the following part of the porter's speech when Macduff, who was asked by Duncan to wake him early, is admitted by the porter and asks him why he has slept so long. The porter replies that he was drunk and had to vomit. His ambiguous jokes about the effects of alcoholic drinks on sex may have amused the audience but they also show his disgusting behaviour, which corresponds to his low mental and social position.

Shakespeare again employs dramatic irony when Macbeth enters and says no to Macduff's question whether the King has already got up. He continues to use irony when Macduff replies to Macbeth's offer to lead him to Duncan that "this is a joyful trouble to you" (line 41). After Macbeth has shown the door to Duncan's room to Macduff, he is asked by Lennox: "Goes the king hence today?" and equivocatingly answers: "He does – he did appoint so" (line 45).

When Macduff has left to wake Duncan, the Thane of Lennox describes the nightly chaos in an apocalyptic way because he not only mentions destruction by storm but also an earthquake, the hooting of the owl, the bird of death, and "strange screams of death" (line 48). Macbeth ambiguously states: "'Twas a rough night," which includes his crime as a deadly sin and the violation of God's order.

Macduff returns with cries of horror and reveals Duncan's murder, which he calls a sacrilege, since in Shakespeare's time the King was considered to be appointed by God. Macduff alarms Duncan's sons and Banquo while Macbeth again pretends not to know that the King is dead and together with Lennox goes to Duncan's room. When Lady Macbeth appears and wishes to know the reason of the noise, Macduff does not want to inform her because that would "murder" her, which again shows Shakespeare's ironical style that he also uses when Macbeth laments: "Had I but died an hour before this chance [misfortune, i. e. the King's death], / I had lived a blessed time" (lines 84–85), which means that he would not have lost his soul to the devil.

When Malcolm wants to know by whom his father was murdered and Lennox casts suspicion on Duncan's bodyguards, Macbeth lies that he killed them in an outburst of rage out of love for the King. Shakespeare underscores Macbeth's lie by his inappropriate use of the word love, which is repeated three times.

Lady Macbeth pretends to faint and Duncan's sons decide to flee, Malcolm to England and Donaldbain to Ireland, because they realise that they cannot trust anybody and fear they might killed, too, whereas Macbeth, Macduff and Banquo decide to investigate the murder.

Scene 4

This scene is connected to the description of the chaotic night of Duncan's murder by Lennox in Scene 3 by an old man and the Thane of Ross, who meet outside Macbeth's castle and talk about the unusual darkness and the unnatural behaviour of animals. In a symbolic way Shakespeare alludes to an owl (Macbeth) that killed a falcon (Duncan). The King's horses ran wild and even ate each other. The old man, who only appears once in this play, seems to express the views of the common people in Shakespeare's time, who believed that the King's murder is mirrored in the chaos of nature, which represents the disturbed universal order.

Macduff appears and tells Ross that Duncan's sons are believed to have bribed the bodyguards to kill their father and have escaped. When Ross explains this behaviour as unnatural and a waste of ambition, Shakespeare also alludes to Macbeth's futile over-ambitiousness. Macduff informs Ross about Duncan's body being taken to Colmkill to be buried there and that he does not want to attend Macbeth's coronation ceremony in Scone, an abbey near Perth, where the Scottish Kings were crowned. As Macduff intends to return to his own castle in Fife instead of going to Scone, he insults Macbeth and thus indirectly shows his suspicion and his disbelief in the accusation of Duncan's sons. At the same time he endangers himself and his family because Macbeth might try to take revenge on him, which he really does later on. The coronation ceremony is not shown on the stage, probably because Shakespeare did not want to confront his patron King James I with the coronation of the murderer of one of his predecessors.

Act 3, Scene 1

At the Royal Palace at Forres, Banquo reflects on the witches' predictions, which have come true for Macbeth. Though Banquo suspects that Macbeth has become king by evil deeds, he hopes that his own descendants will become kings, which the witches had also prophesied.

Macbeth and Lady Macbeth enter the stage for the first time as King and Queen of Scotland and are accompanied by some noblemen. Before Banquo rides off, Macbeth invites him as his "chief guest" to come to his banquet, which Lady Macbeth supports by saying that it would be "a gap" in their great feast if he had been forgotten. Shakespeare again uses the method of dramatic irony, since Banquo will appear at the banquet and fill a gap, i.e. after his death, sitting as a ghost on Macbeth's stool.

Macbeth asks Banquo when and how far he is going to ride, and pretends to want Banquo's advice. He also wants to know whether he is accompanied by his son Fleance. The audience may feel that Macbeth is hypocritically sounding Banquo out because he plans something evil. By Macbeth's words "Fail not our feast" and Banquo's answer "My lord, I will not" (lines 29–30) Shakespeare again alludes to the appearance of the Ghost of Banquo at the banquet in an ironical way. Hypocritically Macbeth tells Banquo that Duncan's sons deny their parricide. Just after saying farewell to Banquo by the ambiguous "God be with you", Macbeth asks a servant whether "those men" have arrived who later turn out to be the murderers who Macbeth has hired to kill Banquo and his son.

Alone, Macbeth expresses the thought that being king is worthless if he cannot be it safely. He fears Banquo's "royalty of nature" (line 51) because he is brave, fearless, loyal, honest and wise and thus qualified to become king himself. In Banquo's presence Macbeth feels repressed and recognises that he has lost his soul, his "eternal jewel" (line 69), to the devil by murdering Duncan only for Banquo's descendants to become kings, since he himself is childless and wears "a fruitless crown" on his head and holds "a barren sceptre" in his hand (lines 62–63). As he wants to prevent that Banquo's descendants become kings, he has hired two murderers, even though he believes in the witches' prophecies. But in spite of that he even decides to challenge fate and fight until his death.

Whereas Duncan's murder was planned by Lady Macbeth, Banquo's and his young son's murder is only planned by Macbeth, whose evil actions are no longer caused by his ambitiousness but by his fear to lose his power. It sounds absurd that he also fears that Banquo's descendants are promised to become kings though he and his wife are childless and thus do not have an heir to the throne. It also sounds absurd that he hopes to defeat fate, which was believed to be impossible in Shakespeare's time.

When the hired murderers enter the stage, Macbeth reminds them of a previous conversation when he persuaded them to believe that not he but Banquo is their enemy and responsible for their misfortune. Thus Macbeth successfully deceives them by several wrong accusations and provokes them to take revenge on Banquo by ridiculing Christian forgiveness and reminding them that they are not dogs but men (as Lady Macbeth did when she urged Macbeth to become a murderer). He pretends that as King he could also punish Banquo, who is their common enemy, but would then run the risk of losing friends, which is the reason why he asked the two men to kill Banquo and his son in a way that nobody will suspect that Macbeth planned the murder.

As they are ready to commit the crime, Macbeth informs them about the place and the time to meet Banquo and his son. The fact that Macbeth knows Banquo's integrity and is convinced that his soul will "find heaven" (line 141) underlines Macbeth's devilish behaviour. His first political decision as King of Scotland is to deceive and urge two men to become murderers.

Scene 2

While Lady Macbeth is alone on the stage, she expresses that she feels isolated, weary and unsafe. She even seems to prefer to be dead than as Queen live "in doubtful joy" (line 9). But as soon as her husband enters, she advises him to forget what cannot be undone. Thus she hides her true thoughts and feelings and pretends to be strong and fearless as she did before Duncan's murder.

Macbeth, however, feels tormented by fear and insecurity and would let the universe fall apart and this life and life after death suffer if he could live without fear and was no longer haunted by terrible dreams. Like his wife, he envies the dead Duncan who is now free from fear and sorrows. Macbeth describes life as a "fitful fever" and enumerates the dangers that no longer threaten Duncan but possibly himself such as treason, murder, civil war and attacks from abroad, which in fact will happen at the end of the play.

Again they decide to feign friendliness and hospitality to their guests, in particular to Banquo. Macbeth does not inform his wife about the assassination attempt on Banquo and his son but only alludes to a terrible deed that she is supposed to approve. As before Duncan's murder when Macbeth asked the stars not to shine at night and to hide his ambition, he now conjures up black night and Hecate's animals of the night. Whereas Lady Macbeth wished the evil spirits to fill her heart before Duncan's murder, Macbeth now imagines in a symbolic way that the evil creatures of night begin to search for their prey like Banquo's murderers. Thus the spectators, who saw the play in the afternoon, were supposed to imagine that the action took place at night.

Lady Macbeth and her husband have changed roles now. Whereas Lady Macbeth was the active character who planned Duncan's murder and urged her husband to kill the King at the beginning of the play, she is now rather passive and asks her husband: "What's to be done?" (line 44), since Macbeth does not inform her about his murderous plan: "Be innocent of the knowledge, dearest chuck" (line 45) and recognises that his wife is amazed by his change: "Thou marvell'st at my words" (line 54). Also Lady Macbeth does not tell her husband how she really feels, which Shakespeare stresses by the rhyming lines of her soliloquy at the beginning of the scene (lines 4 ff):

> Nought's had, all's spent
> Where our desire is got without content.
> 'Tis safer to be that which we destroy
> Than by destruction dwell in doubtful joy.

By characterising Lady Macbeth's and her husband's fears and their envy of Duncan, who has found peace in death, Shakespeare also seems to foreshadow their own death at the end of the play.

Scene 3

At a lonely place near Forres, the two murderers and a mysterious third assassin sent by Macbeth await Banquo and his son at night. The two murderers wonder why Macbeth mistrusts them and has sent a third man. As Banquo and Fleance do not ride but walk the last mile to the castle and are not expecting the murderous attack, they are surprised by the murderers. After unsuspectingly telling the first murderer that it will rain tonight, Banquo is slain by him with the ambiguous and cynical words "Let it come down" (line 18). But the first murderer makes the mistake of extinguishing the torch so that Fleance can escape in the dark after his father's warning and cry for revenge.

Scene 4

In the banqueting hall of the castle, Lady Macbeth and her husband welcome their guests and invite them to take their seats according to their rank. It is the first time that Macbeth and his wife intend to celebrate their reign together with the Scottish noblemen. Whereas Lady Macbeth sits down on her throne to demonstrate her royal position, Macbeth decides to sit in the midst of his noble guests to convey the impression that he is only *primus inter pares* and win his guests' sympathies. At the same time the audience realises that Macbeth and his wife appear separated and no longer cooperating.

Before Macbeth can sit down, the first murderer enters and is pulled aside by Macbeth so that his guests do not notice him or are not able to hear their words. Macbeth asks the murderer to wipe the blood from his face and then learns that Banquo is dead, which he cynically approves by saying: "Thou art the best o'th'cut-throats" (line 17). But when he hears that Fleance has escaped, he is frightened again. He thanks the murderer for his crime and is relieved that at least Banquo is dead, whom he maliciously calls a "grown serpent" whereas his little son, "the worm" (line 29), is not yet old enough to be a danger to him. Contrary to his horror after Duncan's murder, Macbeth is now not at all tormented by his conscience but has become totally heartless and cruel.

When Lady Macbeth reminds him of his ceremonial duties as a host, Macbeth proposes a toast and hypocritically wishes that Banquo would also be present. Shakespeare uses dramatic irony again because Macbeth does not realise that the Ghost of Banquo has already appeared. Macbeth wants to sit down and is horrified by the Ghost sitting on his chair, a sight which can only be seen by him. He asks who has done this, because he at first believes that it is a joke. But when he addresses the Ghost by saying that he cannot accuse him of the deed, Ross invites the guests to rise and leave. Lady Macbeth who tries to control the situation pretends that it is a temporary fit of her husband's that has frequently occurred since his youth but is always soon over.

While the guests are continuing their meal, Lady Macbeth admonishes her husband to "be a man" and overcome his hallucinations by also referring to the "air-drawn dagger" (line 62) which led Macbeth to Duncan as he had believed before. Shakespeare uses dramatic irony again when Lady Macbeth tells her husband: "You look but on a stool" (line 68) while Macbeth is again horrified by Banquo's Ghost who is sitting on that stool. Macbeth is not able to understand why, contrary to former times, the murdered rise again to push him from his seat (cf. lines 75 ff).

As the Ghost has left the stage, Macbeth excuses his behaviour, which he plays down as an illness which he says is nothing unusual to those who know him and proposes another toast to his guests and Banquo, whom he pretends to miss. But during this speech Banquo's Ghost has reappeared and terrifies Macbeth, who tries to scare him off while his wife is appeasing the guests. When Ross asks Macbeth about his visions, Lady Macbeth requests the guests to leave straightaway.

Alone together, Macbeth tells his wife that he has to continue murdering everybody who endangers him, since "blood will have blood" (line 122). He also alludes to Macduff, who did not attend his banquet, and mistrusts all the lords since he has spies in every castle. He then imagines that he stands in the middle of a river of blood where to return is as tiresome as to go on, which means that he has already shed so much blood that to stop now killing people whom he fears would be the same as to go on murdering them:

> I am in blood
> Stepped in so far that should I wade no more,
> Returning were as tedious as go o'er.
>
> (Act 3, Scene 4, lines 136–138)

But he still relies on the weird sisters, who are to tell him about his future even if their prophecies are the worst. He is determined now to reject all other considerations except what is good for him, and will carry out his evil deeds before reflecting on them. Thus he decides to ignore good government, which in Shakespeare's time was believed to be based on careful reflection. He believes that his fear is only the fear of a beginner who lacks experience in doing wrong: "We are yet but young in deed" (line 144). Thus Macbeth is no longer over-ambitious to become king but over-confident to secure his reign as a tyrant.

This banquet scene is the climax of the play because Macbeth and his wife have reached the royal state they want to enjoy and celebrate. But at their climax of power their fall also begins. The banquet scene is also the turning point of the drama, because from now on Macbeth is determined to become a murderous tyrant without distinguishing between good and evil any more. His wife, however, does not really understand Macbeth's decisions and plans when she only says that he lacks sleep. As Macbeth has "murdered sleep" (Act 2, Scene 2, line 45) it is doubtful that he will be able to recover despite his "Come, we'll to sleep" (line 142). After these words Lady Macbeth does not appear on the stage until in the last Act when she is a mad sleepwalker who finally commits suicide.

Scene 5

As it is doubted that this scene was written by Shakespeare, it is frequently omitted in stage performances. Critics believe that Thomas Middleton, a contemporary playwright, who also wrote a play called *The Witches*, is the author of this scene, which, however, is meant to be a link between the former scene and the first scene of Act 4, when Macbeth meets the witches a second time.

Hecate, the witches' mistress, is angry about the three witches who talked to Macbeth without her permission and without giving her the chance to demonstrate her witchcraft. She orders them to meet her and Macbeth in the morning to predict his destiny and mislead him further. Whereas the witches have to prepare their magic tricks and spells, Hecate wants to evoke the apparitions that are meant to totally confuse Macbeth, who rejects fate, despises death and hopes to achieve what is impossible to gain. When she states that "security / Is mortals' chiefest enemy" (lines 32–33), she refers to the previous scene when Macbeth seems to be over-confident and no longer fears failure. But in Shakespeare's time people believed that security meant false security because those who felt secure and were no longer aware of the devil's traps would be ruined by him and end in damnation.

Scene 6

In his castle, the Thane of Lennox and another lord are talking about recent events. In an ironical way, Lennox describes Macbeth's hypocritical behaviour after Duncan's and his bodyguards' death, the false accusation of parricide against the King's sons, Banquo's murder and Fleance as the prime suspect. Lennox does not doubt that Macbeth murdered Duncan, his attendants and Banquo and would also kill Duncan's sons and Fleance if he could seize them.

As Macduff did not attend Macbeth's feast and consequently is also endangered, Lennox wants to know where he is and is informed by the lord that Malcolm has been welcomed at the English Court and that Macduff is also on his way to ask King Edward for troops to support a war against Macbeth to liberate Scotland from the tyrant. When Lennox uses the religious image of a "holy angel" that may fly to the English Court and a "swift blessing" that may return to Scotland's salvation, Macbeth is not only characterised as a tyrant but as a devil. The religious language also implies that the war against him will be a holy war.

Act 4, Scene 1

Shakespeare starts the play with the witches to characterise the main action and promotes it by the second appearance of the weird sisters in the third scene of Act 1. At the beginning of the fourth Act the witches appear for the third time and set the action till the end of the play.

As in the first and third scene of the play, the three witches' appearance is introduced by thunder and they meet at a desolate place near Forres. They move around a cauldron in a magic circle and chant magic songs while throwing poisonous and disgusting ingredients into the boiling soup, e.g. a toad and parts of a snake, bat, dog, dragon, wolf, etc. They even add organs and parts of the bodies of a Jew, Turk, Tartar and a baby that was killed at birth. All the ingredients prove the murderous wickedness of the witches, who had to hurt or kill most of the animals and humans involved in their brew. As Jews, Turks and Tartars are non-Christians, they may also symbolise the prejudices and intolerance of the Christians towards them in Shakespeare's time. According to the witches, the soup or "hell-broth" (line 19) is for Satan and thus also refers to Macbeth's characterisation at the end of the previous scene as a devil.

To stress the magic powers of the witches, Shakespeare uses rhyming couplets, alliteration, and the repetition of the magic number three or thrice, of lines, words, and names, e.g.:

Double, double toil and trouble,
Fire burn and cauldron bubble.
(Act 4, Scene 1, lines 10–11, 20–21, 35–36)

It is doubted whether the appearance of Hecate is Shakespeare's idea. It was probably added by Middleton like the Hecate scene before because Hecate and three other witches do not really promote the action of the play or contribute to its understanding. Hecate only speaks five lines, praises the witches' devilish brew and disappears again.

One of the witches feels "by the pricking of my thumbs" (line 44) that Macbeth is coming, who is called "something wicked" (line 45), which seems to allude to the fact Macbeth is devoid of any human feelings and has become the personification of evil since he is referred to as a "thing" instead of "someone".

Macbeth arrives and contrary to his first meeting when the witches predicted his future without being asked by him, he now demands answers to his questions even if everything is destroyed and the world goes to pieces. He consents to hear his future from the witches' "masters", i.e. from the devil, who appears as three different characters when conjured up by the witches. Since they know Macbeth's thoughts, he is asked not to put questions to them.

The first apparition, "an armed Head", warns Macbeth of Macduff. It is probably a vision of Macbeth's head foretelling his death when he is beheaded by Macduff at the end of the play. The second apparition, "a bloody Child", tells Macbeth that nobody who is born by a woman can harm him. The blood-stained child might symbolise Macduff who was born by caesarean section, which Macbeth only gets to know before he is slain by him. Though he believes now that he need not fear Macduff any longer, Macbeth swears to kill him to make the prediction "double sure".

Finally the third apparition, a crowned child with a tree in his hand, tells him that he will never be defeated until Birnam Wood moves to Dunsinane hill. Thus Malcolm might be shown as Duncan's child who has not yet been crowned King of Scotland and who in Act 5 orders his soldiers to carry branches in front of them to hide their numbers, which to Macbeth appears to be a moving wood.

Macbeth is sure now that such predictions can never come true because he understands the predictions literally without suspecting that they might be ambiguous or allude to his defeat and death, since the apparitions also strengthen his false security by encouraging him to be "bloody, bold and resolute" (line 78) and by telling him that he need not take care (cf. line 89). Macbeth is made to believe that the "armed Head" represents Macduff, since the apparition warns him of Macduff three times, someone Macbeth could kill to get rid of that threat. The second apparition is called more powerful than the first, obviously because the prediction does not require Macbeth to act since he seems to be invulnerable by man. The third apparition tells him something that seems totally impossible to him: "That will never be" (line 93). The apparitions' ambiguity is also confusing because the sequence of their appearance is reversed at the end of the play when first the wood seems to move, then Macbeth learns that Macduff was not "naturally born" and finally Macduff appears with Macbeth's severed head.

When Macbeth wishes to know whether Banquo's descendants will ever become kings, the apparitions disappear without a reply. Instead a procession of eight kings followed by Banquo's Ghost appears, the last king with a mirror in his hand, which shows even more kings. Some of them carry "two-fold balls and treble sceptres", which alludes to Shakespeare's patron King James I, who was crowned King of Scotland before he became King of England and ruled England, Scotland, and Ireland. Then the witches dance and disappear.

When Lennox appears and in reply to Macbeth's question denies that he saw the weird sisters, Macbeth damns "all those that trust them" (line 138) though he must know that at the same time he also damns himself. After Lennox has informed Macbeth about Macduff's flight to England, Macbeth in an aside decides to kill all the members of Macduff's family without hesitation.

Scene 2

In Macduff's castle in Fife, Lady Macduff does not understand what reasons her husband had to flee to England and leave his wife and children unprotected. She doubts whether he loves his family and assumes that he left them because of fear and lack of wisdom. Her cousin, the Thane of Ross, contradicts her suppositions and asks her to be patient. When he alludes to the violent and cruel times they live in, he tells her that Macbeth's tyranny has even destroyed people's integrity. They mistrust each other and are not able to speak frankly. Thus Shakespeare not only explains why Ross does not tell more but also foreshadows Malcolm's behaviour towards Macduff at the English Court in the next scene. After expressing his hope that times will change for the better, Ross leaves.

When Lady Macduff tells her little son that his father is a traitor, he neither believes her nor the murderers who repeat that accusation. Macduff's little son's speech is childlike, and his mother calls him a prattler but he is quick-witted and has probably amused the audience, though Shakespeare uses comic relief again only to emphasise the cruelty of the child's subsequent murder on stage. His mother flees while her son is crying: "Run away, I pray you!" (line 82) but is caught and killed offstage.

Scene 3

Whereas several scenes of the play are very short to promote the action, this scene is the longest and serves to characterise Malcolm, who only appeared in the first Act for a short time and has to be introduced to the audience more closely as the new Scottish King after Macbeth's defeat in the last Act of the play. Moreover, the English King Edward the Confessor is characterised as a pious and good king who supports the "holy war" against the tyrant Macbeth.

In the palace of King Edward, Macduff wants Malcolm to liberate Scotland from Macbeth's tyranny. But Malcolm pretends to be suspicious since Macduff left his family behind and could be Macbeth's secret agent. Like Macbeth, who once was thought honest, Macduff might also be insincere because he has not yet been persecuted by the tyrant. When Macduff begins to despair because he believes that he is unable to convince Malcolm of his honesty and of the need to fight Macbeth, Malcolm continues to test Macduff by telling lies about himself. He pretends to have all the evil traits of a tyrant and as a king would be worse than Macbeth. Macduff cannot believe that "Of horrid hell can come a devil more damned / In evils to top Macbeth" (lines 56–57).

When Malcolm first describes himself as voluptuous and greedy, Macduff tries to play these vices down as less dangerous for the country. But when Malcolm enumerates twelve virtues a king should have such as justice, honesty, generosity, mercy, piety, courage, etc and pretends to be just the opposite and would like to plunge the country into chaos, Macduff despairs and gives up any hope by saying that such a king should not have the right to live. He laments the fate of Scotland and Malcolm's condemnation of himself, which to him is totally incomprehensible because Malcolm is the son of "a most sainted king" (line 109) and a pious mother.

As Malcolm now believes that Macduff's despair is honest, he reveals that he was only testing him by telling lies about himself for the first time in his life. Macduff learns that just the opposite is true, and that Siward, the Earl of Northumberland, and Malcolm himself are ready to fight Macbeth.

A doctor tells that King Edward cures sick people with a touch and has many other God-given abilities, which Malcolm affirms by adding that Edward also has "a heavenly gift of prophecy" (line 159). As Shakespeare characterises Edward the Confessor as an ideal king and God's representative on earth, contrasting his prophetic abilities to the witches' evil predictions, he stresses that the war against Macbeth is also God's will. Moreover, Shakespeare's patron King James I is reminded of an ideal king's virtues and duties.

The Thane of Ross reports that Scotland is terribly oppressed by Macbeth and that those who begin to rise in rebellion against the tyrant must be supported. When Macduff asks Ross about his family the first time, Ross does not tell the truth. Finally however, he confesses that they have been murdered. Macduff is overcome with grief and cannot understand why God did not prevent his family's murder: "Did heaven look on, / And would not take their part?" (lines 226–227). He feels guilty because he left them unprotected but then overcomes his deeply felt grief and wants to take revenge by killing Macbeth, "this fiend [devil] of Scotland" (line 236).

Act 5, Scene 1

In a room in Dunsinane Castle, Lady Macbeth's woman attendant tells the doctor that the queen has been sleepwalking every night since Macbeth left with his army. She gets up, takes a sheet of paper, writes something down, reads it and after sealing it goes to bed again. The audience is neither told what Lady Macbeth is writing nor what she is saying since the gentlewoman is afraid of telling it to anybody. Thus Shakespeare creates suspense before Lady Macbeth appears sleepwalking with a candle in her hand because she is afraid of the dark.

She is rubbing her hands as if washing them and is haunted by the imagination of her and her husband's behaviour and words after Duncan's murder. Contrary to her advice before: "A little water clears us of this deed" (Act 2, Scene 2, line 70), she is now unable to wash the imaginary bloodstains off her hands and thus finally confirms Macbeth's fear when he was looking at his blood-stained hand after having murdered Duncan that all the oceans would not make his hand clean again. She now sighs that "all the perfumes of Arabia will not sweeten this little hand" (lines 42–43). Lady Macbeth repeats fragments of her former behaviour and words and asks herself where Lady Macduff is now. She mentions her admonishing her husband not to ruin their feast when he was horrified by Banquo's Ghost.

Lady Macbeth goes to bed while imagining that she hears the knocking at the gate and is going to bed with her husband after Duncan's murder saying: "what's done cannot be undone" (lines 57–58). Her behaviour and broken language contrast with her self-conscious appearance at the beginning of the play. She is now shown haunted by her crime and mentally disordered, which was already foreshadowed when she admonished her husband not to "think / So brain-sickly of things" (Act 2, Scene 2, lines 48–49) if they should not "make us mad" (line 37). After this scene she does not appear again.

The doctor believes that only God can help her and does not want to talk about what he has seen and heard. When he asks the woman attendant to remove anything with which Lady Macbeth can harm herself, Shakespeare alludes to the danger of suicide, which she really commits as mentioned by Malcolm at the end of the play. Apart from the last lines spoken by the doctor, this scene is written in prose, which underlines Lady Macbeth's madness and her observers' fearful and helpless reaction.

Scene 2

Several Scottish lords and soldiers appear in the open country. The lords talk about the approach of the English army led by Malcolm, Siward and Macduff to Birnam Wood, where they will meet them. Macbeth has fortified Dunsinane Castle and has to face a lot of rebellions against his tyranny. He can no longer rely on his soldiers, who only follow him out of fear. The lords are determined to cure the country by defeating Macbeth and making Malcolm King of Scotland.

Scene 3

In Dunsinane Castle Macbeth rejects the reports about his soldiers defecting to the enemy. He is sure that he is invincible because the apparitions have prophesied events that will never happen: "The mind I sway by and the heart I bear / Shall never sag with doubt nor shake with fear" (lines 9–10). When a frightened servant informs him about the numbers of soldiers of the approaching English army, Macbeth rudely insults him as a coward and furiously orders him to leave. But when Macbeth is alone, he broods over his future and realises that his royal power is at stake now. When he admits that he has "lived long enough" and compares himself to a falling "yellow leaf" in autumn, he seems to believe in his defeat and death. He laments over the loss of honour, love and friendship and is aware of being cursed, flattered only and obeyed out of fear.

When Seyton, his armour bearer, confirms the reports about the advancing English army, Macbeth is determined to fight until death: "I'll fight till from my bones my flesh be hacked" (line 32). He orders that his armour be put on and that everybody should be hanged who talks of fear.

When the doctor tells Macbeth that his wife is suffering from a disease of the mind which he cannot cure, only the patient herself, Macbeth believes that medicine is totally useless but nevertheless asks him to cure her. He no longer wants to hear anything that makes him afraid of death or ruin. When Macbeth has left, the doctor decides to flee without being paid.

Scene 4

Malcolm enters with other lords and soldiers and orders his soldiers to cut branches from the trees to carry in front of them to conceal their numbers when they approach Dunsinane. Thus Malcolm proves to be a clever commander because Macbeth is deceived by this trick of camouflage in the following scene and believes that the prophecy of the third apparition has come true.

Malcolm is sure that Macbeth's only chance is to stay in his castle and try to resist the siege of the English army and that he is not able to risk an open battle since too many soldiers have deserted him.

Scene 5

As Macbeth is still convinced that he is invulnerable, he believes that the enemy will in vain besiege Dunsinane Castle. Hunger and fever will force them to retreat. When women's screams are heard, Macbeth is not startled but only wants to know the reason. When he is told that his wife has died, he only says: "She should have died hereafter; / There would have been a time for such a word" (lines 16–17), which sounds as if he does not care very much. But it might also mean that for the moment there is no time for grief. Nevertheless, his wife's death makes him brood over his life as absolutely meaningless and absurd since his past life has only paved his way to death. He compares life to the light of a short candle, a shadow, a noisy player and a meaningless story:

> And all our yesterdays have lighted fools
> The way to dusty death. Out, out, brief candle,
> Life's but a walking shadow, a poor player
> That struts and frets his hour upon the stage
> And then is heard no more. It is a tale
> Told by an idiot, full of sound and fury
> Signifying nothing.
>
> (Act 5, Scene 5, lines 21–27)

When a messenger reports that Birnam Wood is moving towards Dunsinane, Macbeth begins to doubt the third apparition's prophecy (lines 41–43):

> I pull in resolution and begin
> To doubt th'equivocation of the fiend
> That lies like truth.

Thus the audience is reminded of the ambiguous leitmotif of the play "Fair is foul, and foul is fair" and Banquo's words when he meets the witches at the beginning of the play:

> And oftentimes, to win us to our harm,
> The instruments of darkness tell us truths;
> Win us with honest trifles, to betray's
> In deepest consequence. –
>
> (Act 1, Scene 3, lines 122–125)

But Macbeth realises that too late and admits that he is tired of life. Again he wishes that at the same time also the universe may be destroyed and decides to fight to the death outside the castle.

Scene 6

In this very short scene Malcolm orders his soldiers to throw down the branches and start an open fight to overthrow the tyrant.

Scene 7

Macbeth feels trapped and compares himself to a bear tied to a post that has no other choice but to fight. He still believes in the prophecy of the second apparition that no man born of woman can kill him and fights with Siward's son, who compares Macbeth's name and title to the devil. Macbeth relentlessly slays the young nobleman and feels that the second apparition's prophecy has thus been confirmed.

While Macduff's only desire is to find Macbeth and take revenge on him for his family's death, Old Siward and Malcolm enter Dunsinane Castle, which has been surrendered to the English army since most of Macbeth's soldiers have changed fronts and are fighting on their side.

Scene 8

Though the battle is lost, Macbeth continues fighting because he still believes in the second apparition's words: "I bear a charmèd life which must not yield / To one of woman born" (lines 12–13).

When eventually Macduff finds Macbeth, he calls him a "hell-hound" (line 3). But Macbeth does not want to fight against a man whose family has been murdered by him and who would also be killed by him since Macbeth is still sure that he cannot be defeated by Macduff. Thus Shakespeare does not characterise Macbeth as totally inhuman and as a devil at the end of the play but shows that the tyrant still has some scruples left.

But when Macbeth learns that the prophecy of the second apparition was also ambiguous and false because Macduff was born before he was due, he curses the deceitful devils and their ambiguity:

> And be these juggling fiends no more believed
> That palter with us in a double sense,
> That keep the word of promise to our ear
> And break it to our hope.
>
> (Act 5, Scene 8, lines 19–22)

For a moment Macbeth seems to be disheartened and refuses to fight against Macduff. But when he is called a coward and threatened to be exhibited as a tyrant, he decides to "try the last" (line 32) and is slain by Macduff. Before his death Shakespeare presents Macbeth as a desperately courageous fighter who has recognised at last that he was deceived by the devil and doomed to die. But contrary to the traitor Cawdor at the beginning of the play, Macbeth does not feel remorse for his evil deeds and ends in eternal damnation.

Scene 9

After their victory Malcolm, the lords and soldiers assemble in Dunsinane Castle, where Siward learns that his son has been killed. He does not express his personal feelings or grief but is content when he is told that his son died courageously as "God's soldier" (line 14). Malcolm, however, believes that young Siward is "worth more sorrow" (line 17) and is thus characterised by Shakespeare as a compassionate king who cares for his subjects.

Macduff enters with Macbeth's severed head and hails Malcolm King of Scotland. Malcolm rewards his thanes by making them earls, calls back everybody from exile, and informs his lords and the audience of Lady Macbeth's suicide. Finally he promises to be a good king and invites all of them to see him crowned in Scone.

Thus Shakespeare finishes the play with the liberation of Scotland in a "holy war" and the restoration of political and social order with God's help, "by the grace of Grace" (line 39).

2. The Characters

The list of characters shows that most of them belong to Scotland, a smaller number to England and the smallest number to the supernatural world, which corresponds not only to the frequency of their appearance on stage but also to the fact that this drama is a "Scottish tragedy". The protagonist of the play is Macbeth, who also gives the play its title. But Lady Macbeth can also be called a main character since she decisively contributes to Macbeth's "rise" and fall. Also the three witches, who represent the evil powers that successfully contribute to Macbeth's ruin, play important roles.

While Malcolm, Macduff and to a certain extent also Banquo are Macbeth's most important antagonists, all the other characters are minor characters who play their roles to promote the action or contribute to a more realistic performance or atmosphere of the play.

2.1 Macbeth

Macbeth is a mixed and rather complicated character who is not able to solve his inner conflict between good and evil. He is introduced as a brave nobleman and a loyal adherent of the King of Scotland. But the flaw of his character is his over-ambitiousness, which is used by the witches and his wife to make him a murderer. He is superstitious and lets himself be seduced by the ambiguous "prophecies" of the witches who intend to destroy him, a fact which he is not able to recognise. He is also not strong-willed enough to resist his wife, who persuades him to kill King Duncan by questioning his love and calling him a coward.

At the beginning of the play, Macbeth is introduced by the Captain's report to King Duncan as a brave but also merciless fighter who despises and challenges Fortune and brutally slays the rebel Macdonald, which seems to foreshadow his cruel actions later on and also his being killed and beheaded by Macduff at the end of the play:

> For brave Macbeth – well he deserves that name –
> Disdaining Fortune, with his brandished steel,
> Which smoked with bloody execution,
> Like Valour's minion carved out his passage
> Till he faced the slave,
> Which ne'er shook hands, nor bade farewell to him,
> Till he unseamed him from the nave to th'chaps
> And fixed his head upon our battlements.
> (Act 1, Scene 2, lines 16–23)

When Macbeth enters the stage for the first time, his first words "So foul and fair a day I have not seen" (Act 1, Scene 3, line 36) are nearly the same as the three witches' words in the first scene of the play, who chant the spell:

> Fair is foul, and foul is fair
> Hover through the fog and filthy air.
> (Act 1, Scene 1, lines 12–13)

Macbeth obviously refers to the bad weather when he uses the word "foul", and by "fair" he means his victory. But as the witches express their goal to confuse good and evil by singing their chant, Macbeth already seems to be secretly influenced by them. They intend to make him lose his ability of differentiating between what is good or bad in order to ruin him, which Macbeth does not recognise. He believes that the witches' "prophecy" that he will become Thane of Cawdor has come true when King Duncan greets him by this title. He does not know that King Duncan has already decided to make him Thane of Cawdor. So the witches do not really "prophesy" this but have already known it before they meet Macbeth and thus deceive him into finally believing that their "prophecy" that he will become king may also come true.

> MACBETH [Aside] Glamis, and Thane of Cawdor:
> The greatest is behind.
> (Act 1, Scene 3, lines 115–116)

> MACBETH Two truths are told,
> As happy prologues to the swelling act
> Of the imperial theme.
> (Act 1, Scene 3, lines 126–128)

When the witches disappear and Macbeth says: "Would they had stayed" (Act 1, Scene 3, line 80), he expresses both his wish to know more and his growing dependence on their influence.

But his conscience makes him unsure and he asks himself whether the witches' predictions can be good or bad for him. In his vivid imagination, which is a characteristic trait of Macbeth, he is horrified at the thought that he has to murder Duncan before becoming king himself. Nevertheless he submits to Fortune and wants to accept whatever will happen:

> If chance will have me king, why chance may crown me
> Without my stir.
> […]
> Come what come may,
> […].
>
> (Act 1, Scene 3, lines 142 ff)

As the spectators know Macbeth's true wishes, they realise his dishonesty when meeting King Duncan and feigning loyalty and happiness about the King's wish to come to his castle.

In an aside he is again horror-struck when he imagines that he has to kill Duncan's eldest son Malcolm whom Duncan appointed Prince of Cumberland and his successor to the Scottish throne:

> The Prince of Cumberland: that is a step
> On which I must fall down, or else o'erleap
> For in my way it lies. Stars, hide your fires
> Let not light see my black and deep desires,
> […].
>
> (Act 1, Scene 4, lines 48 ff)

But his conscience is so strong that he feels horrified by the thought of murdering Duncan who is his relative and a guest he is obliged to protect. Though Macbeth knows that Duncan is an extraordinarily virtuous king and that his murder would mean eternal damnation, he at first seems to be unable to overcome his ambition but suddenly decides not to commit the crime when his wife appears: "We will proceed no further in this business" (Act 1, Scene 7, line 31).

But Lady Macbeth is so strong-willed that by referring to his love and courage and informing him about her plan she makes him change his mind and decide to hide his evil designs. He hypocritically tells Banquo that he no longer thinks of the witches and their prophecies (cf. Act 2, Scene 1, line 21).

Macbeth's vivid imagination even makes him have hallucinations when he believes to see a blood-stained dagger that urges him to kill Duncan and seems to lead him the way to the King's room. After the murder he believes he hears voices and is shocked by his inability to say "Amen" in reply to Duncan's servants. He is afraid of returning to them and horrified by the idea that he will never find sleep again:

[…] Macbeth shall sleep no more.
                    (Act 2, Scene 2, line 46)

I am afraid to think what I have done;
[…].
                    (Act 2, Scene 2, lines 54 f.)

Macbeth is terrified by every noise and horrified at himself as a murderer. He wishes that the murder could be undone:

To know my deed, 'twere best not know my self.
                    Knock [*within*]
Wake Duncan with thy knocking: I would thou couldst.
                    (Act 2, Scene 2, lines 76–77)

To hide that he is the murderer, Macbeth feigns that he is innocent, casts suspicion on Duncan's sons, and wrongly accuses Banquo of being the enemy of the two murderers he has hired to kill his friend and his son Fleance. To make sure that the murderers will find their victims Macbeth hypocritically sounds Banquo out to inform the killers about the place and time where they can meet their victims. As Macbeth and his wife are childless, he fears that his regicide, which means the loss of his soul to the Devil, might only have paved the way for Banquo's descendants to become kings. Macbeth behaves in a paradoxical way when he wants to prevent the witches' prophecy to Banquo from coming true and also challenges to fight against him: "[…] come Fate into the list, / And champion me to th'utterance." (Act 3, Scene 1, lines 72–73)

Before Macbeth has planned and done his evil deeds together with his wife, but now he does not fully inform her about the assassination of Banquo. He seems to isolate himself from his wife more and more, though he suffers from nightmares and even envies the peace and security Duncan has found in death. At the banquet with the Scottish thanes, Macbeth has the hallucination of the Ghost of Banquo and is horrified to such an extent that he totally loses control of himself. From now on he intends to kill everybody who might endanger him without any scruples and wants to ask the witches about his future again, even if it would be the worst.

I will tomorrow –
And betimes I will – to the weïrd sisters.
More shall they speak. For now I am bent to know
By the worst means, the worst; for mine own good,
All causes shall give way. I am in blood
Stepped in so far that should I wade no more,
Returning were as tedious as go o'er.
                    (Act 3, Scene 4, lines 132–138)

When he sees the three apparitions, Macbeth is not able to interpret their ambiguous or mysterious predictions properly but continues to trust the spirits. Again he seems to contradict himself when he says to Lennox: "And damned all those that trust them" (Act 4, Scene 1, line 138). According to the second apparition, he need not fear to be killed by someone naturally born, nevertheless he intends to murder Macduff to feel "double sure" (Act 4, Scene 1, line 82). But as the Thane of Fife has gone to England, Macbeth sends murderers to kill Macduff's family. He no longer wants to reflect on his crimes but commit them directly without any scruples:

> From this moment,
> The very firstlings of my heart shall be
> The firstlings of my hand.
> (Act 4, Scene 1, lines 145–147)

But again he also expresses his fear of evil dreams and hallucinations and wishes: "But no more sights." (Act 4, Scene 1, line 154)

Macbeth continues murdering innocent people and sends out spies to every castle because he feels threatened by his lords. Scotland suffers under his extreme tyranny to such an extent that there are the first rebellions. To overthrow the despot, a war is prepared against him by Malcolm, Macduff and the English King. Macbeth, however, feels safe because he believes that "the spirits that know / All mortal consequences" (Act 5, Scene 3, lines 4–5) have told things that can never happen, since everybody is naturally born and a wood cannot move. But in fact he feels tired of life and depressed about his future because of his loss of honour, love and friendship:

> I have lived long enough. My way of life
> Is fall'n into the sere, the yellow leaf,
> And that which should accompany old age
> As honour, love, obedience, troops of friends,
> I must not look to have […].
> (Act 5, Scene 3, lines 22–26)

He continues to feel and behave inconsistently. On the one hand he believes in the spirits' words and decides to "fight till from my bones my flesh be hacked" (Act 5, Scene 3, line 32), but on the other hand he knows that his existence is futile and absurd, stating this after his wife's death, when he compares life to a miserable actor and a meaningless story told by a fool:

> Life's but a walking shadow, a poor player
> That struts and frets his hour upon the stage
> And then is heard no more. It is a tale
> Told by an idiot, full of sound and fury
> Signifying nothing.
> (Act 5, Scene 5, lines 23–27)

Even when he must realise that he was deluded by the third apparition because Birnam Wood really "moves" and he begins "to doubt th'equivocation of the fiend / That lies like truth" (Act 5, Scene 5, line 42–43), he still trusts the second apparition's words until Macduff proves that they are ambiguous and misleading, which Macbeth finally recognises by rejecting them before he is slain by Macduff:

> And be these juggling fiends no more believed
> That palter with us in a double sense,
> That keep the word of promise to our ear
> And break it to our hope.
>
> (Act 5, Scene 8, lines 19–22)

Macbeth is influenced by the witches and his wife to become a murderer. He is not able to resist them and decides himself to fulfil the predictions and to do the evil deed. At the end of the play he curses the witches and recognises their equivocation but does not blame the regicide on them, since it is his own guilt and cause of damnation.

2.2 Lady Macbeth

When Lady Macbeth enters the stage for first time, she is reading her husband's letter about the witches' "prophecies". By her first words she confirms that the prediction of the weird sisters shall come true despite her husband's nature: He is ambitious but does not want to do wrong to achieve his goals. Without hesitation she is at once willing to overcome her husband's moral scruples and persuade him to kill the King.

> Hie thee hither,
> That I may pour my spirits in thine ear
> And chastise with the valour of my tongue
> All that impedes thee from the golden round,
> Which fate and metaphysical aid doth seem
> To have thee crowned withal.
>
> (Act 1, Scene 5, lines 23–28)

Contrary to her husband, Lady Macbeth seems to be strong-willed and unscrupulous. To become even stronger and totally without scruples, she calls upon the evil spirits and implores them to rid her of a woman's kindness and every human feeling to make her cruel and relentless and thus enable her to contribute to the murderous deed.

> Come, you spirits
> That tend on mortal thoughts, unsex me here
> And fill me from the crown to the toe topfull
> Of direst cruelty; […].
>
> (Act 1, Scene 5, lines 38–41)

When Macbeth arrives, she greets him with his titles of Glamis and Cawdor and alludes to his becoming king. She urges him to hide his true intentions and leave the planning of the regicide to her. She is a perfect hypocrite when she welcomes King Duncan and feigns hospitality and kindness.

When Macbeth tells her that he no longer intends to murder Duncan, Lady Macbeth knows how to make her husband change his mind again by doubting his love, manhood and courage. To persuade him totally, she stresses her dire cruelty by telling him that she would even kill her baby if she had sworn to do so. As her husband still fears that the King's assassination could fail, she describes her plan of how to do the evil deed without arousing suspicion and finally persuades him to commit the crime.

Whereas Macbeth is horrified after the murder, Lady Macbeth seems cold-blooded and realistic when she tells him to wash his hands and stop thinking about the deed. But in fact she is not as strong as she pretends to be since she needs alcohol to make her bold. Moreover, the fact that she tells her husband that she would have killed Duncan herself if he had not resembled her father when he slept reveals that she is not devoid of human feelings. She also foreshadows her inability to cope with the murder by saying: "These deeds must not be thought / After these ways; so, it will make us mad." (Act 2, Scene 2, lines 36–37)

In the following scenes she continues to behave hypocritically, and in the Banquet Scene (Act 3, Scene 4) she tries to calm Macbeth and the distrustful lords by telling lies. But when her husband does not inform her about his plan to murder Banquo, she is no longer the predominantly active person but just asks: "What's to be done?" (Act 3, Scene 2, line 44). Finally she appears as a sleepwalking and mad woman who is haunted by the remembrance of Duncan's murder and her guilt (cf. Act 5, Scene 1) before committing suicide.

Whereas Macbeth changes from a conscience-stricken murderer to a desperate killer, Lady Macbeth, who first seems to be unscrupulous, is no longer able to suppress her conscience at the end of the play. Thus Shakespeare does not characterise Macbeth and Lady Macbeth as totally evil but enables the audience to feel compassion for them to a certain extent (cf. Macbeth's soliloquies at the beginning of the play and in Act 5, Scene 1) since both are shown as not strong enough to resist their internal temptation, i.e. their ambitiousness, and the external temptation of the evil powers.

2.3   Banquo and his son Fleance

Like Macbeth, Banquo is a brave combatant, but contrary to Macbeth he remains a loyal subject to King Duncan and is not willing to get involved in the crime (cf. Act 2, Scene 1, lines 26–28). Whereas Macbeth is spellbound after hearing the witches' "prophecy" of his becoming king, Banquo also wants to know what they predict for him, but soon recognises that their predictions are ambiguous and destructive.

> And oftentimes, to win us to our harm,
> The instruments of darkness tell us truths,
> Win us with honest trifles, to betray's
> In deepest consequence.
>
> (Act 1, Scene 3, lines 122–125)

In general Banquo is open-minded towards Macbeth, e.g. when he admits to him that he sometimes thinks of the witches' predictions, whereas Macbeth tells lies to him. Banquo is also too confiding, because he believes that his life is not in danger when Macbeth sounds him out to inform the hired murderers. Though he suspects that Macbeth is involved in Duncan's death, he does not try to verify it but is loyal to the new King, too, and hopes that his own descendants will become kings as prophesied by the weird sisters.

Banquo's son Fleance is a minor character who only appears once on the stage saying a few words. When his father is being attacked and shouts at him to flee and revenge his death, Fleance escapes.

2.4 The Witches, Hecate, and the apparitions

The play begins at a desolate place, obviously the heath, with thunder and lightning, which in Shakespeare's time was believed to be characteristic of witches. They possess evil or poisonous animals such as cats and toads and are able to fly in the air, particularly through fog and mist. They enjoy cooking repulsive soups, in which they throw poisonous and disgusting ingredients while dancing around it and chanting spells. When Banquo meets them, he describes them as thin and dried-up old women with skinny lips and a beard and wearing disorderly clothes. They enjoy doing evil, i.e. destroying things, killing animals and innocent people, and confusing good and evil to spread chaos: "Fair is foul, and foul is fair" (Act 1, Scene 1, line 12).

The witches are also called "weïrd sisters" (*wyrd* is an Old English word for 'fate') and are supposed to be able to predict the future, which referring to Macbeth seems to be true. But since King Duncan makes Macbeth Thane of Cawdor before he meets the witches, they do not really prophesy this but have already got this knowledge in a mysterious way. As they also seem to know Macbeth's ambition and secret wish to become king, they tempt him into ruin by "prophesying" him to become king, which he can only achieve by murdering Duncan as he believes. Their prediction that not Banquo himself but his descendants will become kings seems to be a "true" prediction. But it is assumed that Shakespeare invented this idea to flatter his patron King James I, who believed that Banquo was his ancestor.

Like the witches' predictions, the prophecies of the three apparitions con-

jured up by the witches and called their masters are ambiguous and misleading. They are meant to lull Macbeth into a false sense of security in order to
destroy him finally.

In the play Hecate, six witches and three apparitions or spirits appear. They
all represent evil and are also referred to as powers of the Devil. Whereas
three witches talk to Macbeth twice in the play, once also conjuring up three
apparitions, Hecate and the three other witches do not meet Macbeth. As it
is believed that the verses spoken by Hecate were possibly not written by
Shakespeare but added by his contemporary Thomas Middleton, Scene 5 of
the third Act is frequently left out in modern stage performances. This possibly also applies to Act 4, Scene 1, lines 39–43 when Hecate inappropriately
compares the witches to "elves and fairies".

Hecate, the goddess of witchcraft, appears twice on the stage, the first time
in Act 3, Scene 5 when she blames the three witches because they met Macbeth without asking her. She characterises herself as the witches' mistress of
all evils and wants to prepare the apparitions or spirits to confuse Macbeth
completely by making him over-confident and thus contributing to his ruin.
In Act 4, Scene 1 Hecate appears for the second time and is accompanied by
three other witches. She praises the witches who are going to meet Macbeth
and congratulates them on preparing their disgusting soup.

2.5   King Duncan and his sons Malcolm and Donaldbain

Duncan is shown as a just and generous king when he condemns the traitor
Cawdor and rewards Macbeth with this title for his brave fight and victory.
He is friendly and grateful to Lady Macbeth and through Banquo rewards her
with a ring for her hospitality.

Macbeth knows well that Duncan is a virtuous and gracious king, whose rule
is thought highly of, and that his murder will lead to damnation:

> Besides, this Duncan
> Hath borne his faculties so meek, hath been
> So clear in his great office, that his virtues
> Will plead like angels, trumpet-tongued against
> The deep damnation of his taking-off.
> (Act 1, Scene 7, lines 16–20)

Also Macduff uses religious words when he realises that the King, who was
consecrated as king by God, has been murdered:

> Most sacrilegious murder hath broke ope
> The Lord's anointed temple and stole thence
> The life o'th'building.
> (Act 2, Scene 3, lines 60–62)

But Duncan admits that he is too credulous when he learns that Cawdor is a traitor:

> There's no art
> To find the mind's construction in the face.
> He was a gentleman on whom I built
> An absolute trust.
>
> (Act 1, Scene 4, lines 11–14)

The King is totally guileless and unaware of being in danger when he sees Macbeth's castle and praises its pleasant site (cf. Act 1, Scene 6, line 1). Though he has just been betrayed by Cawdor, whose loyalty he did not doubt, he does not become sceptical but also trusts his murderer Macbeth.

Contrary to their father, Duncan's sons Malcolm and Donaldbain are distrustful and fear that they are in danger after their father's assassination. They decide to flee to different countries, which they believe is safer. Whereas Donaldbain no longer plays a role in the drama, Malcolm, who was appointed Prince of Cumberland and heir to the throne by Duncan, goes to England to win the English King over to fight Macbeth.

Malcolm is very cautious and first treats Macduff like Macbeth's spy and tests his true intentions before he trusts him (cf. Act 4, Scene 3). He is compassionate when he learns that Macduff's wife and children have been murdered and grieves for Siward's son, who was slain by Macbeth, more than his father (cf. Act 5, Scene 9, lines 17–18).

He is determined to liberate Scotland from the tyrant and as he is smart and crafty, he uses the trick of camouflage to hide the number of his soldiers when he orders them to carry boughs in front of them.

The play ends with Malcolm's speech, in which he shows that he will be a virtuous and generous king. Like his father, he rewards his supporters and announces the return of his exiled friends. He wants to rule the country with God's assistance and invites everybody to his coronation ceremony at Scone.

2.6 Macduff and his family

Macduff is loyal to King Duncan and extremely horrified after detecting Duncan's assassination. To him it is a "sacrilegious murder" and "the great doom's image", a picture of the Last Judgement. Macduff is unable to describe what he has seen and looks after Lady Macbeth because he believes that a woman is unable to survive the knowledge of the King's murder and asks someone to help her when she seems to faint.

Macduff seems to be too credulous when he believes that Duncan's sons bribed the King's bodyguards to murder their father. It remains unclear whether he begins to distrust Macbeth when he returns to his home and family refusing to attend the new King's coronation ceremony at Scone (cf. Act 2,

Scene 4, lines 35 ff). But he behaves carelessly or irresponsibly when later on (cf. Act 4, Scene 2) he leaves his family unprotected to go to England to urge Malcolm to overthrow Macbeth's tyranny. Macduff does not expect a king to be without any faults and would excuse such vices as lechery and greed if the king had the royal virtues of justice, truthfulness, generosity, etc to be able to rule the country properly (cf. Act 4, Scene 3).

He feels guilty about leaving his family without being able to save their lives and in his grief he even blames God for letting it happen. But then he swears to take revenge on Macbeth and kill him, which he does at the end of the play. Macduff's wife cannot understand why her husband left her and the children unprotected. To her he appears to be mad or a traitor who does not love her and his children. Macduff's son is an intelligent, quick-witted and courageous boy who warns his mother though he himself is mortally wounded (cf. Act 4, Scene 2).

2.7   Other minor characters and walk-on parts

The list of characters contains 36 characters with a speaking part and additionally a number of walk-on parts. Also according to the title of the play, Macbeth is the most important character who appears in most of the scenes of the play.

The five Scottish Thanes Ross, Lennox, Menteith, Angus and Caithness represent their five territories and are loyal to King Duncan. Most of them are minor characters except perhaps Lennox and Ross, who also describe the terrible events that happened at night while Duncan was murdered. The Thanes are loyal to Macbeth but become suspicious when they observe that the King is frightened by the Ghost of Banquo. Ross comforts Lady Macduff and informs her husband about his family's death. At the end of the play, the Thanes fight against Macbeth and hail the new King.

All the other characters are really minor characters such as the members of Macbeth's household, the Captain, Duncan's younger son Donaldbain, Fleance, Macduff's wife and son, an old man and three hired murderers, Lady Macbeth's gentlewoman and her doctor, Siward and his son, and Seyton, who only appear in one or two scenes of the play and generally have rather short speaking parts. That is why some of the actors could also perform different roles in different scenes.

The minor characters have different functions in the play to promote the action:

– The Captain, who informs Duncan and the audience about the off-stage fight against his enemies, also represents the other brave soldiers of the King's army.
– Donaldbain only appears once when he decides together with his elder brother to flee to different countries.

- The three murderers who are hired by Macbeth to kill Banquo and his son are characterised as gullible, revengeful and cruel.
- Fleance's function in the play is to survive the attempted murder and flee after his father's assassination because he will be the source of the Stuart dynasty.
- Macduff's wife and her son are the innocent victims of Macbeth and contrast to Lady Macbeth and her husband, who are childless.
- The Gentlewoman informs about Lady Macbeth's madness and the doctor has to admit that he cannot help her, whereas the doctor in King Edward's palace (Act 4, Scene 3) reports on the miraculous ability of the King to cure people.
- Siward and his son also embody the courage of the soldiers who fight against Macbeth, though Siward's cold reaction to his son's death only seems to stress Malcolm's compassion.
- Seyton, Macbeth's armour bearer, tells the King that his wife has died.
- The old man in Act 2, Scene 4 testifies the uproar of nature by giving several examples of unnatural events, which mirror Macbeth's crime.

The rather realistic performance of the play is also supported by numerous walk-on parts such as lords, soldiers, attendants, servants, messengers and three more witches, all of them certainly played by a fairly small number of non-professionals.

III Analysis and Interpretation

1. The Sources of the Play

Like all the playwrights in the 16th century such as Thomas Kyd and Christopher Marlowe Shakespeare also knew the medieval *miracle plays* about incidents from the Bible and *morality plays*, which presented the fight of personified Vices and Virtues for the soul of man, as well as classical plays such as the tragedies by the Roman playwright Seneca (4 BC–AD 65), who mainly deals with topics such as murder, revenge, and the apparition of spirits and uses an elaborate style including several soliloquies and moral statements. In *Macbeth* the protagonist is also confronted with the conflict between good and evil, is influenced by witches, reflects on moral conflicts, becomes a murderer, and is finally killed by Macduff in revenge for his evil deeds.

But the most important source of *Macbeth* is Raphael Holinshed's *Chronicles of England, Scotlande and Irelande* (first published 1577), which deal with the early periods of history based on legends and documents. Already as a schoolboy Shakespeare was probably taught history lessons at Stratford Grammar School by reading parts of this book. As a playwright he makes use of the legends and stories told by Holinshed for all his histories, some of the comedies and the tragedies *King Lear* and *Macbeth*. But Shakespeare not only adopts the legendary or historical narrations and their moral evaluations. He uses the second edition of the *Chronicles* (1587) and other sources to select, condense and change the stories and their morals and add new characters, topics and views to them in order to write plays which are supposed to attract a large audience. In particular Shakespeare creates Macbeth's and Lady Macbeth's soliloquies, which give insight into the real motives and conflicts of the characters, as dramatic and psychological masterpieces.

Shakespeare only slightly changes the plot of Holinshed's story for *Macbeth* (cf. Suerbaum, 2001, p. 296–297) and adopts such elements as Macbeth being influenced by the witches and his wife, the murder of Duncan and Banquo, the advance of Birman Wood, etc. But he tightens the action up to create a dramatic sequence of causes and consequences. That is also a reason why this tragedy is Shakespeare's shortest play, in which Macbeth's reign from 1040 to 1057 is condensed to a rapid action of about ten weeks.

The greetings of the witches at the beginning of the play, for instance, are nearly the same in Holinshed's *Chronicles* and in Shakespeare's *Macbeth*:

> All haile, Makbeth, thane of Glammis! Haile, Makbeth, thane of Cawder!
> All haile, Makbeth, that heereafter shalt be king of Scotland!
> (Quoted from: *Shakespeare's Holinshed*, p. 24)

In Shakespeare's *Macbeth*, Banquo is loyal to Duncan, who is a good king, whereas in Holinshed's *Chronicles* Macbeth and Banquo are accomplices and Duncan a weak and incompetent king:

> The woords of the three weird sisters also (of whom before ye haue heard) greatlie incouraged him herevnto [i.e. Duncan's murder], but speciallie his wife lay sore vpon him to attempt the thing, as she that was verie ambitious, burning in vnquenchable desire to beare the name of a queene. At length therefore, communicating his purposed intent with his trustie friends, amongst whome Banquho was the chiefest, vpon confidence of their promised aid, he slue the king at Enuerns [i.e. Inverness] […].
>
> (Quoted from: *Shakespeare's Holinshed*, p. 25)

The family tree of Scottish kings in the 11th century shows that Macbeth had a strong claim to be king, which is also stressed by Holinshed.

Reigns of High Kings of Scotland

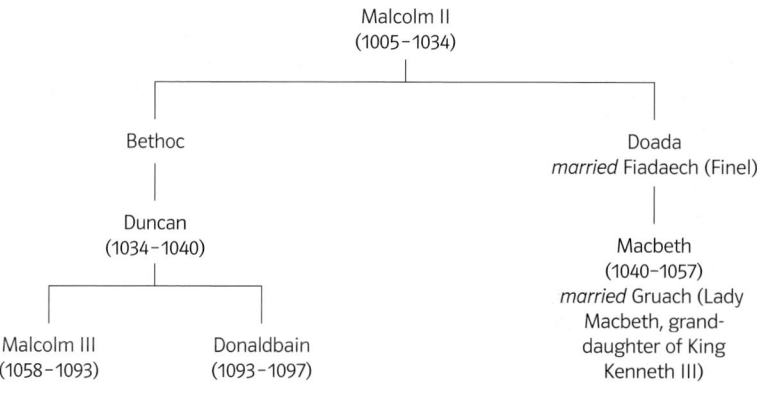

Obviously Shakespeare combined two or three stories told by Holinshed, because in another story the good and pious King Duff is murdered by Donwald, who is his host and who is also urged by his wife, who plans to make the King's servants drunk and to accuse them of the crime. Shakespeare obviously made use of the second story because Holinshed does not tell any particulars of Lady Macbeth's plan and Duncan's murder in the first story. Whereas in Holinshed's *Chronicles* Lady Macbeth is only briefly mentioned as ambitious and as urging her husband to murder the King, Shakespeare presents her as a major character beside Macbeth and for instance invents the sleepwalking scene. In a third story, King Kenneth murders Duff's son and is haunted in his sleep, which might have been a reason why Shakespeare stresses the motif of sleep and sleeplessness in his play.

Superstitious elements such as terrible storms, no sun at daytime and no moon at night, horses eating their own flesh, an owl killing a falcon, etc are also taken from Holinshed's *Chronicles* by Shakespeare in Act 2, Scene 4 as supernatural signs of Duncan's murder.

Holinshed describes Macbeth after the murder as a just and gracious king, who ruled well for ten years before he became a tyrant because of his guilty conscience and fear of being betrayed by Banquo. That is why he hired murderers who killed Banquo like in Shakespeare's *Macbeth*. Nevertheless, he could not overcome his fear of being killed and dethroned like Duncan. Shakespeare, however, condenses time and action and presents Macbeth after Duncan's murder mainly as developing from a conscious-stricken and fearful king to a murderous tyrant.

Banquo, who in Holinshed's chronicle is Macbeth's accomplice, is characterised by Shakespeare as a loyal adherant of the King, which was obviously necessary since Shakespeare wanted to win and keep the sympathies of King James I, the patron of his players' company, who believed that as a Scottish King he was also a descendant of Banquo, the progenitor of the Stuarts. That is why Shakespeare also alludes to James I in Act 4, Scene 1, line 120 by the appearance of several kings who carry "two-fold balls", which James I carried at his two coronations in Scotland and England, "and treble sceptres" which symbolise the three countries England, Scotland and Ireland. Moreover, Shakespeare stresses the roles of the witches, which in the *Chronicles* play a rather unimportant part. The playwright knew that James I was very much interested in witchcraft and had written a book called *Daemonologie* about it, which Shakespeare might have consulted too. The tragedy was probably first performed at the King's Court in 1606 before it was performed in Shakespeare's Globe Theatre. But the first documented performance of *Macbeth* in the Globe based on the report of the astrologer Dr Simon Forman took place in 1611.

2. Setting (Place and Time) and Atmosphere

Shakespeare wrote *Macbeth*, because he wanted to please the King, who was a Scot, with a play that refers to Scotland and its history. Consequently the majority of the characters are Scottish and apart from one scene, all the action takes place in medieval Scotland. The Scottish Thanes represent their territories Ross, Lennox, Angus, Caithness and Fife. Duncan is buried at the traditional place of Colmkill (the Hebridean Isle of Iona) and Macbeth and Malcolm are crowned at Scone, where all Scottish kings were crowned. The following map also shows the Scottish castles such as Forres, Inverness and Dunsinane, where most of the action takes place.

Macbeth's Scotland

Corresponding to the action most of the scenes take place in or near the palace of the Scottish King at Forres, where Duncan is murdered and Macbeth lives as the new King (Act 1, Scenes 1–4; Act 3, Scenes 1–5, and Act 4, Scene 1), at Macbeth's castle in Inverness (Act 1, Scenes 5–7 and Act 2) and in or near Dunsinane Castle, where Macbeth is finally killed (Act 5). Only one scene takes place in the castle of Lennox (Act 3, Scene 6), where Lennox expresses his suspicions, and another scene at the castle of Macduff, where Macduff's wife and son are murdered (Act 4, Scene 2).

There is only one scene in the play which takes place at the English Court (Act 4, Scene 3). But apart from some lines spoken by an English doctor who characterises the English King as a miracle-worker, only the Scottish noblemen Malcolm, Macduff and Ross appear in that scene to prepare the overthrow of Macbeth's tyranny.

As the action of the play only takes place at or near the Scottish noblemen's castles, Scotland appears as a country with several castles and vast parts of waste land and woods without any towns or villages, meadows or fields. The bleak countryside, the heath, is the place where the witches meet. Nothing is said about the Scottish population apart from their suffering under Macbeth's tyranny.

Corresponding to the predominantly evil action most of the scenes take place at night, e.g. when Macbeth murders Duncan, Banquo is killed, the Thanes are invited to Macbeth's banquet, etc. In Shakespeare's time people believed that at night the evil spirits walk and the night is needed by man to do and hide his evil deeds. Thus Banquo calls the witches "instruments of darkness" (Act 1, Scene 3, line 123), Macbeth asks the stars to hide their fires in order to hide his murderous plans (cf. Act 1, Scene 4, lines 50–51) and Lady Macbeth is startled when an attendant tells her that "the king comes here tonight" and she replies, "Thou'rt mad to say it" (Act 1, Scene 5, line 29), because she has already decided to contribute to Duncan's murder. In order not to falter, she invokes both the evil spirits and the night:

> Come, thick night,
> And pall thee in the dunnest smoke of hell,
> That my keen knife see not the wound it makes,
> Nor heaven peep through the blanket of the dark,
> To cry, 'Hold, hold.'
> (Act 1, Scene 5, lines 48–52)

After Macbeth has paved the way to Banquo's murder, he also calls on the night to hide the deed:

> Come, seeling night,
> Scarf up the tender eye of pitiful day
> And with thy bloody and invisible hand
> Cancel and tear to pieces that great bond
> Which keeps me pale. Light thickens,
> And the crow makes wing to th'rooky wood;
> Good things of day begin to droop and drowse,
> Whiles night's black agents to their preys do rouse.
> (Act 3, Scene 2, lines 46–53)

In the last Act of the play Lady Macbeth is haunted by Duncan's murder and as she fears the dark, she has ordered her room to be lit throughout the night while she is sleepwalking.

Even when King Duncan and Banquo praise the lovely site of Macbeth's castle and the pleasant weather (cf. Act 1, Scene 6), the audience knows already that the King will be murdered and therefore cannot really share his feelings.

In most of the scenes of the play the atmosphere is gloomy and dangerous. Before and during Duncan's murder Lady Macbeth, her husband and others are frightened by a shrieking owl, which was believed to be the bird of death and which Lady Macbeth calls "the fatal bellman / Which gives the stern'st good night" (Act 2, Scene 2, lines 3–4). Both the dark spirits and nature mirror the evil, when the witches appear in thunder, lightning, rain, fog and mist. While Duncan is being murdered, nature is in uproar as storms destroy everything, terrible screams are heard and there is even an earthquake as Lennox reports (cf. Act 2, Scene 3, lines 46–53).

3. Motifs

In *Macbeth*, Shakespeare develops certain ideas and topics throughout the play. The most important motifs are Macbeth's and his wife's ambitiousness and lust for power, their moral conflict between good and evil, and the endangering of God's order by chaos.

3.1 Ambition, lust for power, and deep resignation

Whereas Macbeth is a brave and loyal thane at the beginning of the play, his "vaulting ambition" is used by the witches and his wife to urge him to become the King's murderer. Lady Macbeth knows that her husband is ambitious but not willing to do evil to achieve his goals.

> Thou wouldst be great,
> Art not without ambition, but without
> The illness should attend it.
> (Act 1, Scene 5, lines 16–18)

Macbeth is fully aware of this flaw of character but does not know how to take a grip on himself and fears to fail:

> I have no spur
> To prick the sides of my intent, but only
> Vaulting ambition which o'erleaps itself
> And falls on th'other –
> (Act 1, Scene 7, lines 25–28)

Lady Macbeth is only able to urge her husband to murder Duncan after conjuring up the evil spirits that empty her heart of all female feelings and fill it with extreme cruelty:

> Come, you spirits
> That tend on mortal thoughts, unsex me here
> And fill me from the crown to the toe topfull
> Of direst cruelty; […].
> (Act 1, Scene 5, lines 38–41)

She even pretends that she would kill her baby brutally, if she had promised it (cf. Act 1, Scene 7, lines 54 ff) and plays down Duncan's murder by saying: "A little water clears us of this deed" (Act 2, Scene 2, line 70).

But when Macbeth has become king after murdering Duncan, he cannot enjoy his new position. As he fears to lose his power, he continues to murder and sends spies to the castles of his thanes. He becomes a tyrant who is hated and cursed by the people. He is without friends and before his last battle his soldiers defect to the enemy. As he recognises his isolation, he tires of life:

> I have lived long enough. My way of life
> Is fall'n into the sere, the yellow leaf,
> And that which should accompany old age,
> As honour, love, obedience, troops of friends,
> I must not look to have; but in their stead,
> Curses, not loud but deep, [...].
>> (Act 5, Scene 3, lines 22–27)

When he is informed of his wife's death, Macbeth recognises his life's futility
and absurdity:

> [Life] is a tale
> Told by an idiot, full of sound and fury
> Signifying nothing.
>> (Act 5, Scene 5, lines 25–27)

Macbeth does not even care if the universe is destroyed when he dies:

> I 'gin to be aweary of the sun
> And wish th'estate o'th'world were now undone.
>> (Act 5, Scene 5, lines 48–49)

Lady Macbeth, who tries to feign complete control of their situation, goes
mad when she is haunted by her crime and no longer able to suppress her
conscience, finally committing suicide.

3.2 Moral conflict between good and evil

The witches' moral paradox "Fair is foul, and foul is fair" is echoed by Macbeth's first words when he comes on the stage for the first time. This con-
fusion of good and evil, which is intended by the witches to destroy man,
is the leitmotif of the whole play. As *fair* also means "beautiful" and *foul*
"ugly", Macbeth certainly means the weather when he uses the word *foul*,
and comments on his victory with the word *fair*. But at the same time he
is already characterised by Shakespeare as being under the influence of the
witches without being aware of it. His rise and fall is already contained in the
witches' chant.

At the beginning of the play Macbeth is neither good nor evil. He is good
because he defends his King against a traitor and he is bad because of his
over-ambitiousness. But he is aware of the difference between good and evil
and follows his conscience.

When he hears the witches' predictions, he begins to doubt: "This supernatural soliciting / Cannot be ill, cannot be good" (Act, 1, Scene 3, lines 129–130).
Though he is horrified by the idea of murdering Duncan, he does not decide
to refrain from becoming king. Instead he is weak-willed and surrenders to
Fate, i.e. the witches' intention to ruin him:

> If chance will have me king, why chance may crown me
> Without my stir.
> [...]
> Come what come may,
> [...].
>> (Act 1, Scene 3, lines 142 ff)

As the witches and his wife know his weakness, they successfully urge Macbeth to become a murderer. He is not strong enough to resist the witches' ambiguous predictions and his wife's questioning his love, manhood and courage. But he is not their puppet since he has to choose between good and evil himself and to decide to commit the regicide or refrain from the evil deed.

Whereas Lady Macbeth calls for the evil spirits to fill her heart with unnatural cruelty and suppresses her conscience, Macbeth's conscience makes him consider what to do. But after his wife's challenge of his manhood, he is determined to murder Duncan and following the hallucination of a blood-stained dagger he commits the crime without considering the moral implications and consequences: "I go, and it is done" (Act 2, Scene 1, line 62).

But immediately after the deed, Macbeth is conscience-stricken:

> I am afraid to think what I have done;
> Look on't again, I dare not.
>> (Act 2, Scene 2, line 54–55)

> To know my deed, 'twere best not know my self.
>> *Knock [within]*
> Wake Duncan with thy knocking: I would thou couldst.
>> (Act 2, Scene 2, lines 76–77)

He is horrified by the murder and believes that Duncan's blood cannot be washed from his hand but will rather colour the oceans red, whereas Lady Macbeth only advises him to wash his hands and to stop thinking: "Be not lost / So poorly in your thoughts" (Act 2, Scene 2, lines 74–75).

He is also horrified by the idea that he will never be able to sleep again because by murdering the sleeping King, he believes that he "murdered sleep" (cf. Act 2, Scene 2, line 45). Lady Macbeth, who seems to be extremely cruel at the beginning of the play, does not feel able to kill Duncan herself since he resembled her father as he slept (cf. Act 2, Scene 2, lines 12–13). After the deed, Macbeth is haunted by nightmares and at the end of the play Lady Macbeth is shown sleepwalking and brain-sick.

When the apparitions predict that "none of woman born shall harm" Macbeth and he cannot be defeated unless Birnam Wood moves to Dunsinane, he is convinced that "that will never be" (Act 4, Scene 1, line 93) and believes that he is invincible. But already a short time after this prophecy when he talks to Lennox, he curses everybody who trusts the witches (cf. Act 4,

Scene 1, line 138), which he contradicts again when he seems to be convinced that the spirits "know / All mortal consequences" (Act 5, Scene 3, lines 4–5). Macbeth is as insecure and inconsistent as the witches' predictions until he finally doubts the ambiguous predictions of "the fiend [devil] / That lies like truth" (Act 5, Scene 5, lines 42–43) like Banquo at the beginning of the play (cf. Act 1, Scene 3, lines 121 ff).

Contrary to Macbeth, Banquo is not tempted into wrongdoing either by the witches or by Macbeth. He remains loyal to the King because he does not want to lose his honour (cf. Act 2, Scene 1, lines 25 ff).

3.3 The Elizabethan belief in a universal order threatened by chaos

3.3.1 God's order and chaos

In Shakespeare's time, people believed in God and a life after death in Heaven. They believed in a God-given universal order from God's throne down to the elements, liquids and metals. Man's place in this chain is between the angels and animals with spiritual and carnal qualities. But this order is permanently threatened by the devil and his evil spirits such as the witches that try to urge man to do evil and plunge him into hell and the world into chaos.

The characters in *Macbeth* frequently refer to God when they need his help, express good wishes or greet each other. Macbeth is horrified when after Duncan's murder he is not able to repeat the word "Amen" used by Duncan's praying servants. He also knows that he has lost his soul, his "eternal jewel", to the devil, "the common enemy of man" (Act 3, Scene 1, line 69 f).

Banquo believes that the witches are ministers of the devil (cf. Act 1, Scene 3, line 105), Macduff calls Macbeth a "hell-hound" (Act 5, Scene 8, line 3), Young Siward associates Macbeth's name with the devil and hell (cf. Act 5, Scene 7, lines 7–9) and Malcolm calls Macbeth "devilish" (Act 4, Scene 3, line 117) and his wife a "fiend-like", i.e. devilish, queen (Act 5, Scene 9, line 36). When the porter of Macbeth's castle says: "But this place is too cold for hell. I'll devil-porter it no further" (Act 2, Scene 3, lines 13–14), Shakespeare seems to identify the castle with hell and Macbeth with the devil.

In *Macbeth*, Shakespeare shows this universal conflict by Macbeth's murder of a good and gracious king, whose right to rule the country is believed to be God-given. Macbeth's violation of God's universal order is mirrored in the uproar of nature and the unnatural behaviour of animals:

> The night has been unruly: where we lay,
> Our chimneys were blown down, and, as they say,
> Lamentings heard i'th'air, strange screams of death
> And prophesying with accents terrible
> Of dire combustion and confused events,

[…].
                    Some say, the earth
        Was feverous and did shake.
                              (Act 2, Scene 3, lines 46–53)

Also Ross and an old man describe the same night as chaotic. Though it is already daytime, the sun is obscured. Against its nature an owl (symbolising Macbeth) killed a falcon (symbolising Duncan) and Duncan's obedient horses suddenly became wild and ate each other. Thus not only has Macbeth destroyed the God-given order but so, too, have animals "as they would make war with mankind" (cf. Act 2, Scene 4, lines 10–18). At the end of this scene the old man bids Ross farewell and wishes that God's order would be restored:

        God's benison go with you, and with those
        That would make good of bad, and friends of foes.
                              (Act 2, Scene 4, lines 40–41)

In place of all his brave and fallen soldiers, Malcolm mourns Young Siward, who was slain by Macbeth, by also referring to God and Siward calls his dead son God's soldier (cf. Act 5, Scene 9, lines 20 and 14).

At the end of the play, Malcolm is hailed as the rightful King of Scotland, who in the name of God, "by the grace of Grace" (Act 5, Scene 9, line 39) demonstrates royal virtues and goes to Scone to be crowned. According to God's universal order, the King is by God's will the highest worldly authority who must be obeyed. Thus the murder of a good king such as Duncan is sacrilegious, whereas the fight against a tyrant like Macbeth is legal, just and called a "holy war".

In *Macbeth*, the English King Edward the Confessor is characterised as the ideal king by Malcolm, who enumerates the King's qualities such as justice, truthfulness, moderation, firmness, generosity, humility, faithfulness, courage and constancy (cf. Act 4, Scene 3, lines 91 ff.). The Doctor and Malcolm even praise King Edward's ability to cure people by his touch and that he has – contrary to the evil predictions of the witches – "a heavenly gift of prophecy" (line 159).

By alluding to the seven deadly sins ("every sin"), Malcolm characterises Macbeth and every tyrant as murderous, lustful, greedy, faithless, deceitful, violent, and malicious (cf. Act 4, Scene 3, lines 57–60). As Macbeth was performed at the Court of James I, Shakespeare also seems to be reminding the King of his qualities and duties.

At the end of *Macbeth*, the violation of order is overcome and God's order restored, which is achieved by the victory of Malcolm's and Macduff's troops and the English King's army, the tyrant's death and the coronation of Malcolm as the rightful and gracious new King.

3.3.2 Fate and Fortune

Though the Elizabethans believed in God and the existence of the devil, they also believed in fate, which was uncertain since Fortune, the goddess of fate, was fickle and unreliable. Because of the mutability and unpredictability of Fortune, man's life was believed to be a chain of ups and downs as shown in *Macbeth*. The personification of Fate and Fortune stresses their power.

At the beginning of the play, the Captain calls Fortune a "whore", who first seems to take sides with Duncan's traitor but is disdained by Macbeth during the fight (cf. Act 1, Scene 2, lines 14 ff).

Also Macbeth knows that the fate predicted to him by the witches "cannot be ill, cannot be good" (Act 1, Scene 3, line 130). As he is afraid of becoming active himself and murdering Duncan to become king, he seems to surrender to fate (cf. Act 1, Scene 3, 142–143) by saying: "Come what come may" (Act 1, Scene 3, line 145). But when he is king and fears being threatened by Banquo, he intends to fight until death by challenging fate and thus overrates human abilities:

> [...] come Fate into the list,
> And champion me to th'utterance.
> (Act 3, Scene 1, lines 72–73)

Macduff's feelings of revenge are so strong that he implores Fortune to let him find Macbeth, which as he says is his only wish (cf. Act 5, Scene 7, lines 23–24).

According to the rotation of the Wheel of Fortune, Duncan is first on top of it but then murdered by Macbeth whose turn it is now to reach the top of power only to be ruined at the end of the play with Malcolm rising to the top. Though Malcolm's fate is not presented in the play, the critical spectator might doubt whether his restoration of justice and order will last and if the chain of violence has really come to an end.

4. Form and Structure

In the First Folio, the full title of the play is *The Tragedy of Macbeth*. According to Aristotle, a tragedy in ancient Greece is defined as a play that purges the spectator through pity and fear of these emotions, which he calls "catharsis". The protagonist, e. g. *Oedipus* by Sophocles, is misled by the oracle of the gods and finally ruined because he tries to evade their inhuman prediction that he would kill his father and marry his mother. His life is tragic because in trying to prevent the crimes he unknowingly commits them.

Compared with the ancient Greek tragedy, Macbeth is not a tragic character in the classical sense because he can decide himself whether to become a murderer or remain innocent. The Shakespearean tragedy is based on Macbeth's flaw of character, his over-ambitiousness and inability to resist the evil influence of his wife and the misleading predictions of the witches until his death. But despite his guilty conscience, he finally makes up his mind to murder Duncan: "I go, and it is done" (Act 2, Scene 1, line 62).

The Elizabethan tragedy was mainly influenced by Seneca, who deals with the most horrific traditional topics, subdivides his tragedies into five Acts with a climax and a kind of moral shock effect at the end. By contrast to Seneca, Shakespeare finishes *Macbeth* with the restoration of order after the tyrant's death.

Shakespeare's plays are divided into five Acts like the classical plays by Seneca. But contrary to the classical three unities of time, place and action, the Acts in Shakespeare's plays fall into a different number of scenes of different length. The actions take place at various places and different times. Like Christopher Marlowe, Shakespeare employs blank verse, i.e. lines of five iambic feet (pentameter) without a rhyme. In *Macbeth*, only the witches use rhyming tetrameters, which stress their magic powers and their chanting spells.

The Porter uses prose by which Shakespeare underlines the character's low social and moral position. Also Macbeth employs prose once when he speaks to the murderers he hired to kill Banquo (cf. Act 3, Scene 1, lines 77 ff) and thus underlines his moral and social fall. Prose is also used by Lady Macbeth when reading her husband's letter and in the sleepwalking scene to underline the Queen's madness. Her Gentlewoman and the Doctor, in parts, employ prose, which underscores their fear. Shakespeare switches from verse to prose when Lady Macduff and her son change to a child-like conversation.

Since there were no curtains at the front stage which could be closed when an act or a scene ends, Shakespeare sometimes uses rhyming couplets (two-liners) at the end to signal to the audience that a scene or act is over, in particular if this is not evident from the action or the words used by the actors. As Act 3, Scene 3 for instance ends: "Well, let's away, and say how much is done" there are no final rhyming couplets. Sometimes rhyming couplets are also used at the beginning of a scene or within a scene, for instance to stress Macbeth's strong belief in the third apparition's prophecy: "Such a one / Am I to fear, or none" (Act 5, Scene 7, lines 3–4).

As the Elizabethan theatres were rather small with the groundlings standing tightly packed, there was a rather close intimacy between the actors and the audience. This is why Shakespeare frequently uses asides or soliloquies in his plays, which inform the audience about the secret thoughts and feelings of a character, while it is assumed that the other characters cannot hear them and know less than the spectators. Macbeth's soliloquies mirror his inner conflicts and thus draw the spectators' attention to the moral problems of the play, the inner or interior action, whereas the exterior action becomes less important than it was in Shakespeare's early play *Titus Andronicus*. This might also be the reason why in *Macbeth* Duncan's and Lady Macduff's murders and Lady Macbeth's suicide are not shown on stage. It might also be that Shakespeare did not want to confront his patron James I with the murder of a Scottish King on stage. On the other hand, Macbeth's cruelty is stressed by the murder of Banquo and Macduff's little son and when Young Siward is slain by Macbeth on the open stage.

Shakespeare not only uses end-stopped lines but frequently enjambement. He divides up the lines of a dialogue into two or more parts spoken by different characters to increase the dramatic effect, particularly by the use of stichomythia, when a line is split up in several short segments, for instance to underline Macbeth's and Lady Macbeth's excitement after Duncan's murder:

> LADY MACBETH Did not you speak?
> MACBETH When?
> LADY MACBETH Now.
> MACBETH As I descended?
> LADY MACBETH Ay.
>
> (Act 2, Scene 2, lines 16–20)

The structure of the play mirrors the development of its tension:

– In the first Act, the exposition, the audience is introduced to the place, time and main action of the drama. It begins with the leitmotif of the play "Fair is foul, and foul is fair" and arouses the audience's suspense by the mysterious atmosphere and Macbeth's and Lady Macbeth's intention to murder Duncan.

– The rising action in the second Act leads to Duncan's murder and the escape of his sons.

– In the third Act the action reaches its climax when Lady Macbeth and her husband want to celebrate their reign at a banquet with the Scottish noblemen and Macbeth is terrified by the Ghost of Banquo. It is also the turning point of the play because from now on Macbeth suffers a change from being a powerful king to becoming a hated tyrant.

– The falling action of the fourth Act is introduced by the predictions of the apparitions and informs the audience about Macduff's motif of revenge and the preparations for the war against Macbeth at the English Court. Thus the play's tension is reduced because the spectators can foresee Macbeth's defeat. But as they do not yet know how this will happen due to the apparitions' predictions, they are still kept in suspense.

– The fifth Act presents the mental and physical ruin of Lady Macbeth, her husband's justified death and the restoration of order by the new King. Thus the ending of the play is not a classical tragic catastrophe for the protagonist but a denouement, in which the conflict between good and evil is settled. The audience's suspense gradually diminishes as the apparitions' predictions come true one after the other.

The structure of the play

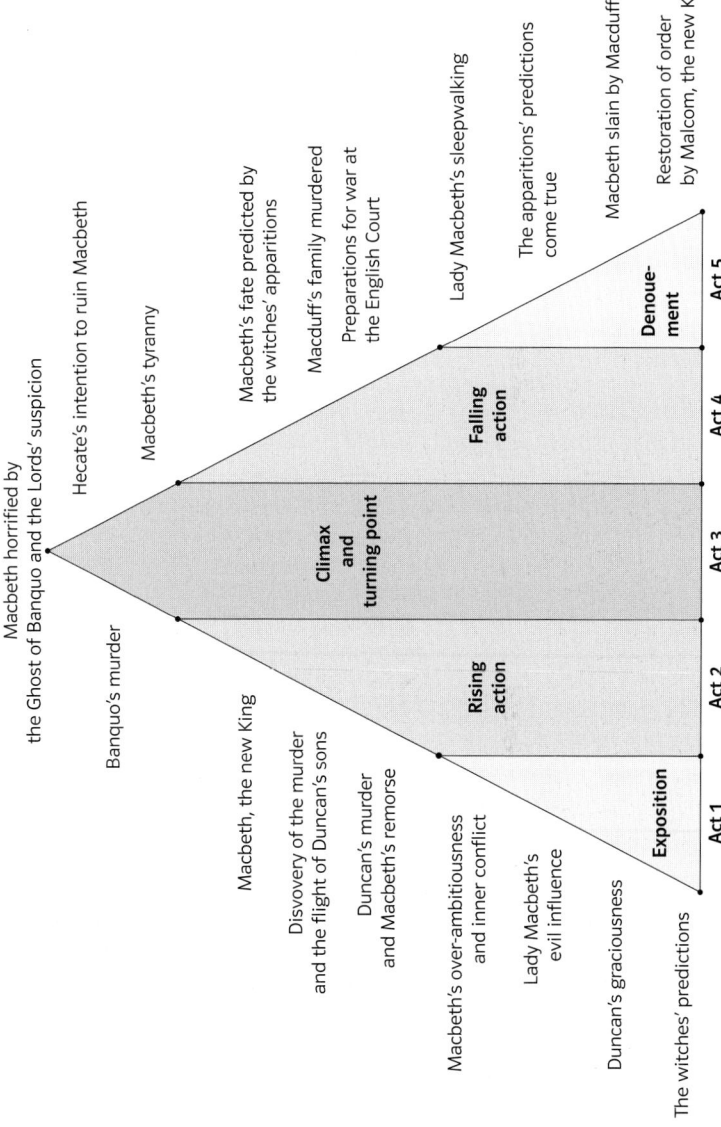

The witches' predictions

Duncan's graciousness

Lady Macbeth's evil influence

Macbeth's over-ambitiousness and inner conflict

Exposition

Act 1

Duncan's murder and Macbeth's remorse

Discovery of the murder and the flight of Duncan's sons

Macbeth, the new King

Rising action

Act 2

Banquo's murder

Macbeth horrified by the Ghost of Banquo and the Lords' suspicion

Climax and turning point

Act 3

Hecate's intention to ruin Macbeth

Macbeth's tyranny

Macbeth's fate predicted by the witches' apparitions

Macduff's family murdered

Preparations for war at the English Court

Falling action

Act 4

Lady Macbeth's sleepwalking

The apparitions' predictions come true

Macbeth slain by Macduff

Restoration of order by Malcom, the new King

Denouement

Act 5

Whereas the sketch on p. 71 reflects the dramatic tension of the play on a large scale, the audiences' suspense is kept throughout the play by Macbeth's soliloquies before and after the murder, by the sequence of battles or murders throughout the play, by the witches' and apparitions' predictions coming true one after the other and by the references to Macbeth's hallucinations, supernatural events, Banquo's Ghost and Lady Macbeth's madness.

The following sketch visualises these elements of suspense with the battle of a good king at the beginning of the play and the final battle at its end, which reflects the circular structure of the tragedy.

Elements of suspense

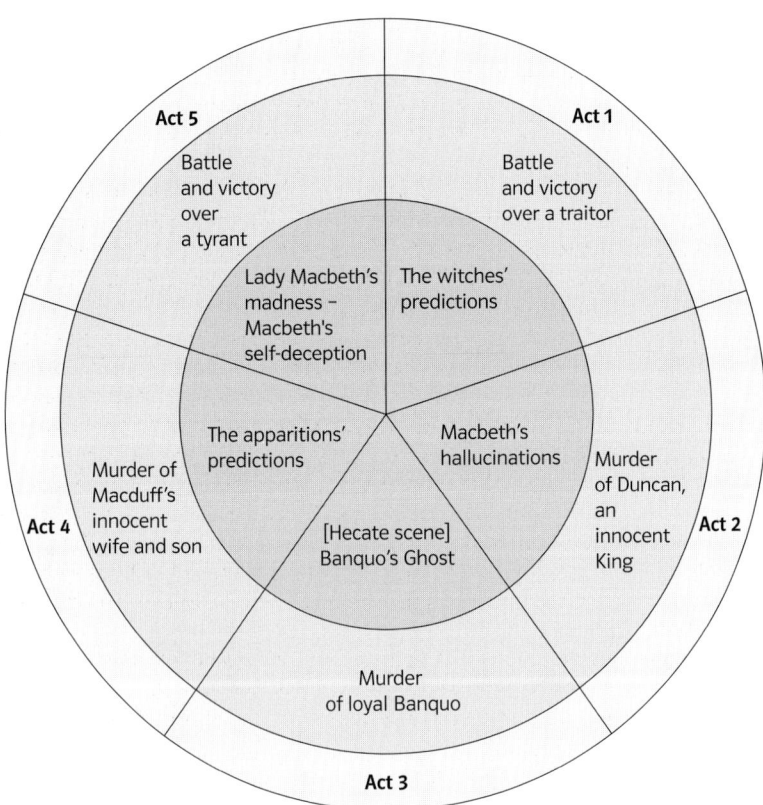

5.   Shakespeare's Language

The language used by Shakespeare reflects the change of the English language since the Elizabethan time. Because of the differences between Shakespeare's English and modern English, his plays can only be understood even by an English audience if the language of the plays is more or less adapted to its present use as it is done in modern stage performances or films.

The readers who want to read a Shakespearean play in the original language have to use a Shakespeare lexicon, a glossary, notes or a study guide if they want to be sure of the meaning of an obsolete word, for instance, though its meaning can sometimes also be derived from the context.

There are the following main language differences in Shakespeare's *Macbeth*:

1. Obsolete words or change of meaning such as paddock (toad), anon (at once), broil (battle), favour (face), dudgeon (handle), benison (blessing), quell (slaughter, murder), incarnadine (make blood-red), limbeck (skull), missive (messenger), mated (confused), illness (wickedness), sightless (invisible), sooth (truth), etc.

2. Old use: hither (to this place), thither (to or towards that place), Hark! (Listen!); old use or literary: ere (before), nought (nothing); old use or dialect: thou (you, subject case), thee (you, object case), thy (your) and thine (your, before a vowel), ye (you, plural); old-fashioned: foe (enemy), old-fashioned or humorous: tidings (news), quoth (said)

3. Shakespeare sometimes differentiates between the personal pronouns *we* and *I* and *you* and *thou* to stress their different social usage: King Duncan uses the royal plural *we* and *our* to underline his royal position but e.g. changes to "I" to express his personal gratitude to Macbeth for his victory. King Duncan is respectfully addressed by *you/your* (cf. Act 1, Scene 4, lines 23, 25; Scene 6, lines 19, 26), which he also politely employs when he meets his hostess Lady Macbeth (cf. Act 1, Scene 6, lines 13 ff.) But *thou* is generally used and indicates familiarity or (social) inferiority of the person addressed. Lady Macduff changes from *you* to *thou*, when she talks to her little son and calls him a "prattler", obviously to underline his child-like talk (cf. Act 4, Scene 2).

4. Archaic verb forms: Second person singular: [thou] art (are), dost (do), didst (did), shalt (shall), shouldst (should), wouldst (would), couldst (could), canst (cannot), mayst (may); third person singular: [it] seemeth (seems); hath (has); doth (does)

5. Questions and negatives without using *do* or *did*: "And when goes hence?" (Act 1, Scene 5, line 57); "Know you not, he has?" (Act 1, Scene 7, line 30); "went it not so?" (Act 1, Scene 3, line 85); "How goes the night?" (Act 2, Scene 1, line 1); "Ride you this afternoon?" (Act 3, Scene 1, line 19); "I think not of them" (Act 2, Scene 1, line 21); "Go not my horse the better"

(Act 3, Scene 1, line 26); "regard him not" (Act 3, Scene 4, line 58); "I know him not" (Act 4, Scene 3, line162).

6. Use of the subjunctive: "If he do bleed" (Act 2, Scene 2, line 58).

7. Adverbs are sometimes used with or without the ending -ly, e.g. "which the false man does easy" (Act 2, Scene 3, line130).

8. Sometimes Shakespeare employs double negation for emphasis, e.g. when Macduff finds Duncan dead: "Tongue nor heart / Cannot conceive nor name thee" (Act 2, Scene 3, line 57).

6. Shakespeare's Dramatic and Stylistic Devices

6.1 Foreshadowing and reviewing

By alluding to future action and looking back on former events, Shakespeare establishes a relationship between the various acts and scenes of his play, which enhances its impact on the audience and demands attentive spectators.

When the Captain reports on Macbeth's victory and describes Macbeth as "disdaining Fortune" (Act 1, Scene 2; line 17), he anticipates Macbeth's "come Fate into the list" (Act 3, Scene 1, line 72). Macbeth foreshadows his will to fight until death by saying: "And champion me to th'utterance" (Act 3, Scene 1, line 73), which he repeats in other words at the end of the play: "They have tied me to a stake; I cannot fly, / But bear-like I must fight the course" (Act 5, Scene 7, lines 1–2) and "Yet I will try the last" (Act 5, Scene 9, line 32).

The first witch wants to torment a sailor by preventing him from sleeping "neither night nor day" (Act 1, Scene 3, line 18) and thus foreshadows Macbeth's fear of being unable to sleep after murdering the sleeping King: "Methought I heard a voice cry, 'Sleep no more: / Macbeth does murder sleep'" (Act 2, Scene 2, lines 38–39).

Lady Macbeth, who knows her husband's character very well, foretells how he will react after Duncan's murder when she says what he fears he wishes "should be undone" (Act 1, Scene 5, line 23), which Macbeth confirms after the evil deed:

> To know my deed, 'twere best not know my self.
> *Knock [within]*
> Wake Duncan with thy knocking: I would thou couldst.
> (Act 2, Scene 2, lines 76–77)

Macduff, who finally kills Macbeth, foreshadows the tyrant's death by saying: "Front to front / Bring thou this fiend of Scotland and myself; / Within my sword's length set him" (Act 4, Scene 3, lines 235 ff). And Macbeth himself also foresees his death when he begins to "doubt th'equivocation of the fiend [the devil] / That lies like truth" (Act 5, Scene 5, line 42–43).

Macbeth frequently reminds the audience of the witches' and apparitions' predictions, and Lady Macbeth rebukes her husband by ridiculing his hallucination of "the air-drawn dagger which you said / Led you to Duncan" (Act 3, Scene 4, lines 62–63) when he is horrified by the Ghost of Banquo.

At the end of the play, Lady Macbeth is sleepwalking and permanently trying to wash her hands in vain. Thus Shakespeare reminds the audience of her words after Duncan's murder: "A little water clears us of this deed" (Act 2, Scene 2, line 70). By repeating various sentences she used after Duncan's and Banquo's murder, Lady Macbeth shows that she is haunted by her crime and has become mad, which was foreshadowed by her several times before, e.g. when an attendant announces the arrival of King Duncan, Lady Macbeth spontaneously answers: "Thou'rt mad to say it" (Act 1, Scene 5, line 29) and after the murder of the King she replies: "A foolish thought" (Act 2, Scene 2, line 24) when her husband is shocked by Duncan's blood on his hands. Macbeth is horrified by his inability to say "Amen" after the murder. But his wife only gives the advice: "These deeds must not be thought / After these ways; so it will make us mad" (lines 36–37) and: "Be not lost / So poorly in your thoughts" (line 74–75). When Macbeth believes that he will never sleep again, his wife replies that he should not "think so brain-sickly of things" (lines 48–49).

6.2   Dramatic irony, ambiguity, paradox; comic relief and puns

Dramatic irony and ambiguous speech is most characteristic of Shakespeare's language in *Macbeth*. Nothing seems to be as it appears to be. Dramatic irony also enables the audience to be better informed about what is true than the characters of the play and can arouse suspense since the spectators are aware of the characters' inappropriate behaviour.

The leitmotif of the play, the witches' paradoxical spell "Fair is foul, and foul is fair", i.e. the mixing of truth and lie, is also characteristic of man's behaviour in *Macbeth*, e.g. when Macbeth reflects on the witches' predictions:

This supernatural soliciting
Cannot be ill, cannot be good.
(Act 1, Scene 3, lines 129–130)

Shakespeare employs dramatic irony to characterise Macbeth by using nearly the same words as the witches when he appears on the stage for the first time: "So foul and fair a day I have not seen" (Act 1, Scene 3, line 36).

Dramatic irony is also used when Duncan admits that he absolutely relied on the traitor Cawdor and realises that "there's no art / To find the mind's construction in the face" (Act 1, Scene 4, lines 11–12), but immediately after that trusts Macbeth, his murderer, and Lady Macbeth, who feigns a friendly welcome and hospitality.

When Duncan admires the lovely location of Macbeth's castle and Banquo mentions a martin which has built its nest in the castle wall because it feels safe there (cf. Act 1, Scene 6), just the opposite is true concerning the King. When Macbeth tells his wife: "Duncan comes here tonight" (Act 1, Scene 5, line 57) and she asks him when the King will leave again, Macbeth answers ambiguously: "Tomorrow, as he purposes" (line 58).

At Macbeth's banquet, the Ghost of Banquo has already entered the scene while Macbeth twice regrets that Banquo has not yet arrived: "Were the graced person of our Banquo present" (Act 3, Scene 4, line 41) and "Would he were here" (line 91). When he is asked by Ross to sit down, he is shocked by the Ghost of Banquo, who is sitting on his stool. As nobody apart from Macbeth and the audience sees the Ghost of Banquo, Lady Macbeth's words to her husband "You look but on a stool" (Act 3, Scene 4, line 68) contribute to the dramatic irony of the play and might have also aroused the audience's laughter.

The representatives of ambiguity are the witches and the apparitions that prophesy things in "a double sense, / That keep the word of promise to our ear / And break it to our hope" (Act 5, Scene 8, lines 20–22), as Macbeth finally recognises. Because of the second apparition's prediction that no man who was born of a woman could kill him, Macbeth feels safe but must realise that it was not mentioned that Macduff was born by caesarean section.

Ambiguous speech is also characteristic of Macbeth when he asks Banquo's murderers if "Banquo's safe" (Act 3, Scene 4, line 25), i.e. dead. Even Malcolm pretends that he would be a vicious king and thus drives Macduff to despair until he admits that it is not true (cf. Act 4, Scene 3).

While dramatic irony is not meant to amuse the audience, it can have a comic effect, too (e.g. Macbeth's reaction to the Ghost of Banquo), comic relief as a dramatic means is used in *Macbeth* to alleviate the tragic effect for a while in order to arouse it all the more later, e.g. by the bawdy language of Macbeth's porter (Act 2, Scene 3), who crudely refers to sex. But the porter, who calls himself the porter of Hell, is not really able to amuse the spectators since they know that Duncan has been killed just before the porter appears on stage. As the audience also knows that Macduff's family will be murdered, the child-like talk of Macduff's son (Act 4, Scene 2) is not really comic, which also applies to puns such as "Fathered he is, and yet he is fatherless" (line 27) or "Whom we, to gain our peace, have sent to peace" (Act 3, Scene 2, line 20), referring to Duncan's murder.

6.3   Imagery

Shakespeare employs a lot of images, metaphors and comparisons to visualise and stress the dramatic action and produce pictures in the minds of his audience, which also help them to imagine events which they do not see performed on stage. Most of the images, metaphors and comparisons refer to evil and chaos, nature and man's life, religion and order. They are taken from different fields such as war, crime, death, religion, witchcraft, nature, animals, hunting, clothes, sickness, medicine, etc.

Evil and chaos

To stress evil and chaos, Shakespeare makes use of his knowledge of ancient Greek and Roman mythology and history also to evoke images mainly in his educated spectators' minds, e.g. by mentioning Acheron (one of the rivers of the underworld in ancient Greek), auguries (in ancient Rome prophecies based on the observation of birds), Bellona (Roman goddess of war, wife of Mars), Gorgon (horrible ancient Greek creature who could change anyone that looked at her into stone), Harpy (in Greek mythology a cruel monster with a woman's body and a bird's wings and claws), Hecate (ancient Greek goddess of the underworld and witchcraft), Neptune (ancient Greek god of the sea), oracles (in ancient Greece the gods' answers about the future), Mark Antony and Caesar (referring to ambitiousness), the Roman fool (in ancient Rome a soldier dying on his sword after the battle was lost was believed to die honourably), Tarquin (Roman prince who raped Lucrece).

Several images visualise the relationship or analogy between man and cosmic order or disorder. Macbeth for instance implores the stars to hide their fires so that his murderous ambition cannot be seen (cf. Act 1, Scene 4, line 50–51). The chaotic night of Duncan's murder is described by an apocalyptic image of destruction:

> The night has been unruly: where we lay,
> Our chimneys were blown down, and, as they say,
> Lamentings heard i'th'air, strange screams of death
> And prophesying with accents terrible
> Of dire combustion and confused events,
> New hatched to th'woeful time. The obscure bird
> Clamoured the livelong night. Some say, the earth
> Was feverous and did shake.
>
> (Act 2, Scene 3, lines 46–53)

When Donaldbain recognises the false smiles of Macbeth and Lady Macbeth, Shakespeare uses a metaphor instead: "There's daggers in men's smiles" (Act 2, Scene 3, line 133).

Shakespeare frequently uses metaphors and images of blood, e.g. referring to the bloodshed in battle and murder throughout the play. Macbeth sees himself in the middle of a river of blood and broods on going on murdering:

                    I am in blood
    Stepped in so far that should I wade no more,
    Returning were as tedious as go o'er.
                    (Act 3, Scene 4, lines 136–138)

The colours of red, black and white are frequently used symbolically. Red referring to blood symbolises murder and death, black refers to murder, evil and chaos, and white to fear in connection with white things such as lily, linen, whey, snow (cf. e.g. Act 3, Scene 4, line 116; Act 5, Scene 3, lines 14 ff). White things like milk or snow are generally not employed to emphasise purity or innocence but rather the opposite, e.g. when Lady Macbeth calls on the evil spirits to change her milk to gall (cf. Act 1, Scene 5, line 46) or when Malcolm tests Macduff by wishing to "pour the sweet milk of concord into hell" (Act 4, Scene 3, line 98) or "black Macbeth" is ironically described as "pure as snow" (lines 52–53).

Nature and man's life

After the King's murder Mabeth praises sleep, which he personifies, by using an image and a sequence of metaphors:

    Sleep that knits up the ravelled sleeve of care,
    The death of each day's life, sore labour's bath,
    Balm of hurt minds, great nature's second course,
    Chief nourisher in life's feast.
                    (Act 2, Scene 2, lines 40–43)

To stress the bloody deed and to increase the impact on the audience, Shakespeare uses an exaggerating image of the ocean:

    Will all great Neptune's ocean wash this blood
    Clean from my hand ? No: this my hand will rather
    The multitudinous seas incarnadine,
    Making the green one red.
                    (Act 2, Scene 2, lines 63–66)

Similarly to the use of venomous or dangerous animals such as snakes and toads, bats, dragons, wolves and sharks in connection with the witches (cf. Act 4, Scene1), Shakespeare also employs images referring to poisonous or dangerous animals, e.g. the snake, when Lady Macbeth advises Macbeth to hide his true thoughts and feelings from Duncan: "[…] look like th'innocent flower, / But be the serpent under't" (Act 1, Scene 5, lines 63–64).
The image of a poisonous snake and of a scorpion is used when the malicious Macbeth fears being threatened by Banquo:

> We have scorched the snake, not killed it;
> She'll close, and be herself, whilst our poor malice
> Remains in danger of her former tooth.
>
> (Act 3, Scene 2, lines 13–15)

> O, full of scorpions is my mind, dear wife!
>
> (Act 3, Scene 2, line 36)

When Banquo is murdered and Fleance has escaped, Macbeth again uses the image of snakes, calling the dead Banquo a grown serpent and his son a "worm" (little snake) that "will venom breed", but has "no teeth for th'present" (Act 3, Scene 4, lines 29–31).

Macbeth alludes to Banquo's death by using images of night animals, which were believed to be sent by the witches:

> […] ere the bat hath flown
> His cloistered flight, ere to black Hecate's summons
> The shard-born beetle with his drowsy hums
> hath rung night's yawning peal, there shall be done
> A deed of dreadful note.
>
> (Act 3, Scene 2, lines 40–44)

Whereas the witches make use of poisonous plants like hemlock and yew, Macbeth demands – in a metaphorical way – that his country should be purged by rhubarb and cynne (cf. Act 5, Scene 4, line 56). Thus Shakespeare likes to refer to sickness and medicine, also when he uses the metaphor of fever for earthquake (cf. Act 2, Scene 3, line 53).

Personification is used e.g. referring to sleep (cf. Act 2, Scene 2, lines 39 ff) or to night, presented as an image of death:

> Come, seeling night,
> Scarf up the tender eye of pitiful day
> And with thy bloody, and invisible hand
> Cancel and tear to pieces that great bond
> Which keeps me pale. Light thickens,
> And the crow makes wing to th'rooky wood;
> Good things of day begin to droop and drowse,
> Whiles night's black agents to their preys do rouse.
>
> (Act 3, Scene 2, lines 46–53)

A lot of metaphors refer to nature or man, such as "the seeds of time" for the future (Act 1, Scene 3, line 56), "the seeds of Banquo" for his descendants (Act 3, Scene 1, line 71), "chickens" for children and "dam" for mother (Act 4, Scene 3, line 220), "the travelling lamp" instead of sun (Act 2, Scene 4, line 7), "fruitless crown" and "barren sceptre" for Macbeth's childlessness (Act 3, Scene 1, lines 62–63), "common eye" instead of public view (line 124) and "crown" for head (Act 3, Scene 4, line 81), "our mother" and "our grave" for Scotland (Act 4, Scene 3, line168).

Clothes are often not literally referred to but symbolise man's thoughts and action, e.g. when Lady Macbeth tells Macbeth to put on his "night-gown" ('Hausgewand') to be prepared to demonstrate their alibi when they are called (cf. Act 2, Scene 2, line 73). Macduff expresses his suspicion by saying: "our old robes sit easier than our new" (Act 2, Scene 4, line 39) and thus refers to Duncan's good reign and Macbeth's reign based on an evil deed.

When he talks to Banquo's murderers, Macbeth compares different men to the different races of dogs (cf. Act 3, Scene 1, lines 91 ff). Certain animals are associated with the night such as owls and crickets. Some animals are symbols of death such as the raven (cf. Act 1, Scene 5, line 36), in particular the owl, which is also called the "fatal bellman" (Act 2, Scene 2, line 3) or "the obscure bird" (Act 2, Scene 3, line 51) and the kite a symbol of hell (cf. Act 4, Scene 3, line 219).

The noble falcon symbolises King Duncan, whereas his murderer is symbolised by an owl (cf. Act 2, Scene 4, lines 12 f). Man is compared to certain animals that symbolise various virtues, for example to courageous animals such as eagles, lions (cf. Act 1, Scene 2, line 35), and bears (cf. Act 5, Scene 7, line 2), even to the wren that defends itself against the owl (cf. Act 4, Scene 2, lines 9 ff). Cowards are compared to animals that stand for fear such as sparrows, hares (cf. Act 1, Scene 2, line 35) and geese (cf. Act 5, Scene 3, line 13).

The frequent and loud knocking on the castle's gate at night symbolises the knocking of death on man's door (cf. Act 2, Scenes 2 and 3), which Macbeth wishes would wake the King he has murdered (cf. Act 2, Scene 2, line 77) and which intensifies the impact on the audience.

Like in the medieval morality plays, Shakespeare uses allegories, e.g. Fortune (Act 1, Scene 2, line 17), Fate (Act 3, Scene 1, line 72) and "the even-handed justice", i.e. a woman with scales in one hand and a sword in the other (Act 1, Scene 7, line 10). Also the line of kings in Act 4, Scene 1 is presented in an allegorical way.

Shakespeare likes to intensify his words by combining several stylistic devices such as repetition, alliteration, images and metaphors, e.g. when referring to Macbeth's despair in his impressive last soliloquy:

> Tomorrow, and tomorrow, and tomorrow
> Creeps in this petty pace from day to day
> [...]
> The way to dusty death. Out, out, brief candle,
> Life's but a walking shadow, a poor player
> That struts and frets his hour upon the stage
> And then is heard no more. It is a tale
> Told by an idiot, full of sound and fury
> Signifying nothing.
>
> (Act 5, Scene 5, lines 18 ff)

As in the miracle plays, the images used by Shakespeare are sometimes far-fetched and not easy to understand, though skilful and combined with other stylistic devices such as antithesis. Such a conceit is used by Macbeth before Duncan's murder when he would like to catch the consequences of the murder with a net:

> If th'assassination
> Could trammel up the consequences and catch
> With his surcease success […].
> (Act 1, Scene 7, lines 2 ff)

Religion and order

As Shakespeare knew the medieval miracle plays that present incidents of the Bible, he employs several elements of these plays such as Heaven, angels, Golgotha, the devil, hell and the porter of hell-gate. He also refers to the Bible, e.g. when Macduff characterises Malcolm's pious mother who "died every day she lived" (Act 4, Scene 3, line 111), which according to I Corinthians XV, verse 31 means that a Christian should die daily to sin.

Shakespeare uses numerous religious metaphors, e.g. when the King's dead body is called "The Lord's anointed temple" (Act 2, Scene 3, line 61) or "the great doom's image" (line 72) and man's soul the "eternal jewel" (Act 3, Scene 1, line 69).

Religious words are used again and again throughout the play, such as God or Grace, devil/devilish, fiend-like, angel (once in the sense of fallen angel, i.e. devil), Christendom, church, holy, pious, prayer, Amen, benison, blessing, benediction, sacrilegious, sainted, miraculous, divine, merciful, sin, sinful, damned, blaspheme.

6.4 Rhetorical devices

In order to stress the words of the characters, Shakespeare frequently uses such poetic devices as antithesis, hyperbole, alliteration, repetition, enumeration and parallelism.

As the conflict between good and evil is most characteristic of his tragedy *Macbeth*, Shakespeare frequently uses antithesis to stress it. The witches' "Fair is foul, and foul is fair" is supposed to be a very strong spell because of its antithetical structure, which is even intensified by its alliteration and the use of chiasm (reversed repetition of words). Also Macbeth's conflict is frequently stressed in his soliloquies by the use of antithesis, combined with repetition, e.g.:

> This supernatural soliciting
> Cannot be ill, cannot be good. If ill,
> [...]
> If good [...].
>
> (Act 1, Scene 3, lines 129–133)

The antithesis between the dagger he sees and his suspicion that it is "a dagger of the mind" (Act 2, Scene 1, lines 33 ff) emphasises his hallucination. Lady Macbeth for instance advises her husband to "look like th'innocent flower, / But be the serpent under't" (Act 1, Scene 5, lines 63–64), which is visualised by the use of an image and stressed by antithesis. Thus Shakespeare likes to demonstrate his poetic skill by combining several stylistic devices as he also does when Malcolm pretends that in comparison to himself "black Macbeth / Will seem as pure as snow" (Act 4, Scene 3, lines 52–53).

By hyperbole (exaggeration) Shakespeare for instance stresses Macbeth's horror when he looks at his bloody hands:

> Will all great Neptune's ocean wash this blood
> Clean from my hand? No: this my hand will rather
> The multitudinous seas incarnadine,
> Making the green one red.
>
> (Act 2, Scene 2, lines 63–66)

When Macbeth meets the murderers of Banquo, Shakespeare emphasises his fears by the use of alliteration: "But now I am cabined, cribbed, confined, [...] / To saucy doubts and fears" (Act 3, Scene 4, lines 24–25). Alliteration is frequently used to stress an idea, e.g. fitful fever; fill full; carried to Colmkill; fail not our feast; dusty death; day to day; beard to beard; beat them backward.

By repetition the words of the witches are meant to be magic (cf. Act 1, Scene 1; Act 4, Scene 1). Lady Macbeth seems to resemble the witches when she magically calls upon the evil spirits by repeating the verb "come" three times (cf. Act 1, Scene 5, lines 38, 45, 48). Repetition combined with alliteration is for instance used to stress Macbeth's intention: "The very firstlings of my heart be / The firstlings of my hand" (Act 4, Scene 1, lines 146–147) or to underscore his bloodthirsty plans: "It will have blood they say: blood will have blood" (Act 3, Scene 4, line 122). Macduff's alliterative repetition underlines his despair by "Bleed, bleed, poor country" (Act 4, Scene 3, line 31).

Enumeration is e.g. used to list the disgusting ingredients of the witches' broth and to underline the vices and virtues of kings (cf. Act 4, Scene 3). Parallelism stresses e.g. the opposite attitude of Malcolm and Siward towards Young Siward's death: "He's worth more sorrow, / [...] He's worth no more" (Act 5, Scene 9, lines 17–18).

The New Globe Theatre in London

IV Adaptations of Shakespeare's *Macbeth*

Since the first performance of Shakespeare's *Macbeth* in 1606, the play has fascinated audiences, readers, producers, stage and film directors, writers, composers, cartoonists, and last but not least teachers and students throughout the world. This may be the reason why there are numerous adaptations of *Macbeth* that follow more or less the original play. Particularly modern versions are sometimes rather experimental and heavily disputed whereas performances that strictly follow Shakespeare's text are also criticised as out of date.

Shakespeare festivals attract audiences worldwide and several Shakespearean plays on film have become blockbusters. The following examples can only give an incomplete survey of the great variety of the adaptations.

1. Stage Productions

After the closing down of the theatres by the Puritans in 1642, Shakespeare's plays were also no longer performed until the theatres were reopened in 1660. But contrary to the audience from all social strata in Shakespeare's time, the aristocracy appreciated more refined performances, stage equipment and machinery. Shakespeare's *Macbeth*, which had already been altered soon after Shakespeare wrote it, e. g. by Thomas Middleton, was permanently adapted to the new demands, i. e. rewritten and changed to such an extent that it did not have very much in common with the text published in the First Folio in 1623, which is probably not totally Shakespeare's original text since there is no early print.

William Davenant's operatic adaptation of *Macbeth* (1664) with comic shows of dancing and singing witches was very successfully performed until the 18th century, and even in 1864 for instance more than 100 actors performed the songs and dances. With the exception of David Garrick's psychologically oriented presentation of Macbeth's character most of the other performances of the play were rather declamatory or – to attract more spectators – spectacular. The acting editions continued to differ more or less from the edited collections of Shakespeare's plays until the 19th century. In the 20th century the performances became less lavish and more authentic.

The Old Vic Theatre, London, which opened in 1818, has had a great influence on the history of drama and was the first theatre to perform the complete works of Shakespeare as a series. Nowadays the Royal Shakespeare Company's performances in London and the annual Shakespeare festival at the Royal Shakespeare Theatre in Stratford-upon-Avon are authentic attempts at taking Shakespeare's original words seriously, which also applies to most of the performances at other theatres in England such as the Compass Theatre Company in Sheffield, even if they performed *Macbeth* in 1987 with only six actors who had to play up to seven different parts virtually without any stage equipment.

As Shakespeare's plays including *Macbeth* are performed worldwide either in the original language, in modern English or the native language of the respective country, the words of Shakespeare's friend Ben Jonson have come true: "He was not of an age but for all time." This also applies to the Royal Shakespeare Company's one year festival in Stratford-upon-Avon, which started on Shakespeare's birthday in 2006. At the festival the complete works of Shakespeare including the narrative poems and the sonnets were performed on the three stages of the town, and several theatre companies from Japan, South Africa, India and Sri Lanka, Iraq, the USA and Germany were invited to present their stage productions. *Macbeth* was performed by a play group from Poland.

At the end of the 16th century Shakespeare's plays were performed by English travelling players' companies in Germany for the first time. The first performances were in English at courts and markets without sticking to the original texts but stressing comic and external effects such as gesticulation, emotionalism and brawl. In the 18th century when, after the predominance of the French classical plays by Corneille and Racine, Shakespeare's works were praised by the German classical writers such as Lessing, Herder, Goethe and Schiller as model plays for German dramatists and were translated into German first by Wieland in prose (1762–66) and then by the romantic writers August Wilhelm Schlegel, Ludwig and Dorothea Tieck and Wolf Graf Baudissin (1797–1825) followed by numerous translations until the 20th century, *Macbeth* has also frequently been performed in German. Like Dr Johnson, who defended Shakespeare's disregard of the three unities of time, place and action, the German *Sturm und Drang* and classical dramatists also neglected these unities and wrote plays whose action did not consist of a single plot taking place at a single location on one day only. The plays have been performed according to the Schlegel-Tieck version, or based on "modern" translations or in experimental ways.

Whereas in his *Macbeth* Friedrich Schiller for instance replaces the porter's bawdy words by a pious morning song, Heiner Müller's *Macbeth* adaptation (1982) focuses on Scotland as an abattoir based on a wrong social order. The adaptation by Düsseldorf Schauspielhaus in 2005 presents a naked and blood-smeared Macbeth, which was rejected by a large part of the audience as scandalous and disgraceful. But because of its radical interpretation of violence and the actors' great theatrical achievement, the company was invited to Munich, Vienna, the Netherlands and Berlin Theatre festival (2006). Such performances may be heavily disputed but they also prove that Shakespeare's plays are still alive, and the former director of the Royal Shakespeare Theatre Company in Stratford-upon-Avon is still right when he wrote in 1964 "There is no Final Shakespeare."

The performances of Shakespeare's plays at the reconstructed Globe Theatre (see picture on p. 83), which was built nearly on the same site in London (on the South Bank of the Thames in Southwark) as Shakespeare's Globe and was opened in 1996, have attracted millions of spectators who wish to be taken back to Elizabethan England. That is why other Globe Theatres were built, e.g. in Neuss (1991) and Tokyo (1988) though the latter building does not much resemble Shakespeare's Globe.

2. Film Productions

In addition to Shakespeare's words "All the world's a stage" one could say "… and a screen". There are more than 250 cinematic adaptations of Shakespearean plays and also some adaptations of *Macbeth*.

Scene from Orson Welles' "Macbeth" (1947): Macbeth (Orson Welles) reclines at the dinner table as Lady Macbeth (Jeanette Nolan) and several courtiers look on.

Orson Welles, the director of *Citizen Kane* (1941), which according to film critics is the best film of all times, is both the director and the protagonist of *Macbeth* (1947), a black-and-white movie that seems to have been entirely shot at night. "The scenario includes inspired additions, deletions, and transpositions of all sorts and varieties," e. g. "a dialogue overlap, Macbeth is dictating the first part of the letter to Lady Macbeth, who then is suddenly seen at the castle reading the last half aloud" (Rothwell, 2004, p. 71). The low-key lighting, the dark atmosphere, the skewed camera angles and the close-ups of the characters lay stress on Macbeth's conflict between good and evil, his ambition and remorse and his wife's excessive ambition. Low-angle shots are frequently used to underscore Macbeth's powerful position. As Banquo's Ghost is only seen by Macbeth, it emerges, disappears and re-emerges in the banquet scene. Orson Welles presents Macbeth in an impressive and highly intense way.

Akira Kurosawa (*Throne of Blood*, also known as *Spider's Web Castle*, 1957) seems to follow Orson Welles' sinister *Macbeth* adaptation but transposes the action of the play from medieval Scotland to medieval feudal Japan with castles, forests and samurais and makes use of the stylistic means of the Japanese No-Theatre such as wildly exaggerated facial play and gestures. Kurosawa does not show extended samurai slaughter but focuses on the characters. His *Macbeth* is one of his most famous films and was nominated for the Golden Lion at the Film Festival in Venice in 1957.

Roman Polanski shot *Macbeth* in 1970/71 after his pregnant wife Sharon Tate had been murdered in 1969 by the clan of Charles Manson, who was driven by his pathological lust for murder. This might have been the most important reason for Polanski to shoot an extremely violent and bloody film that visualises cruel scenes which in Shakespeare's play take place offstage. Whereas Shakespeare frequently uses images of blood, Polanski extensively shows violence and bloodshed in a naturalistic way. The film begins with the brutal execution of the Thane of Cawdor. Duncan's murder is presented on-screen as a shocking bloodbath and Macbeth's severed head is extensively shown at the end of the play. Polanski also changes the role of Ross, who is the third murderer, and lets the murderers of Macduff's family enter the castle. He only makes use of about 40% of Shakespeare's play and presents a lot of images and sounds that resemble a horror film. "This is Theatre of Cruelty – a demonic universe of whips, gibbets, and scaffolds. The violence, as Polanski himself would argue, is not gratuitous but necessary: 'if you don't show violence the way it is, I think that's immoral and harmful'" (Weinraub, "Interview with Polanski, 1971", quoted after: Rothwell, 2004, p. 149).

Contrary to Shakespeare's play, Polanski's film does not end with the restoration of order by the new King but stresses the continuation of violence and murder. Whereas in Shakespeare's *Macbeth*, Malcolm's brother Donaldbain disappears from the stage after his escape to Ireland, in Polanski's film he

Portrayal of the Macbeths (Scene from Polanski's "Macbeth" with Jon Finch and Francesca Annis, 1971)

returns to the witches to ask for their prophecies and seems to be planning to murder his brother Malcolm, the new King – "in a cyclical pattern of evil" (Rothwell, p. 151).

Alexander Abela's *Makibefo* (2000) is set in a fishing village in Madagascar. There the ambitious protagonist is urged by his wife to murder the good King after the prediction of a sorcerer, though he first hesitates because of his moral conflict. Thus central ideas taken from Shakespeare's *Macbeth* are transposed to Africa. The non-professional actors are inhabitants of Madagascar and have to improvise their roles to a certain extent.

There are several TV movies, e.g. the Thames TV version (1978) of Trevor Nunn's highly acclaimed Stratford stage production (1976) with minimal props and the rather lavish BBC movie as part of the Shakespeare television series of all his plays (Director: Jack Gold, 1983), which conveys the impression of a filmed stage production.

Some other *Macbeth* film adaptations more or less retain Shakespeare's words but are set in the underworld of gangsters such as *Joe MacBeth* (1955), the Mafia film *Men of Respect* (1991), the Indian gangster film Maqbool (2004) or Geoffrey Wright's Australian adaptation *M* (2006). *Scotland, PA* (2001) is a Macbeth adaptation as a black comedy and Allison L. Licalsi's *Macbeth – The*

Comedy (2001), which presents a female Macbeth and mixes contemporary dialogue with the original language of the play, is a fun movie and is meant to appeal to a wide audience that does not understand Shakespearean English very well.

3. Various other *Macbeth* Adaptations

Shakespeare's *Macbeth* has also inspired composers, writers, dramatists, painters, cartoonists, illustrators, advertisers, etc (cf. also *http://en.wikipedia. org/wiki/Macbeth*).

Giuseppe Verdi for instance composed the first version of his opera *Macbetto* in 1847 and Richard Strauss the tone poem *Macbeth* in 1890. Dimitri Shostakovich's opera *Lady Macbeth of Mtsensk* (1930–32) is not based on Shakespeare's play but on a Russian novelette and is set in a bourgeois milieu with a murderous female protagonist. The albums *Thane of the Throne* (2000) by Jag Panzer and *A Tragedy of Steel* (2002) by Rebellion might appeal to younger people.

Several sinister sketches and paintings of Macbeth and Lady Macbeth with blood-stained hands and the witches were for instance produced by the Swiss Johann Heinrich Füssli (called Henry Fuseli in his London exile, 1764).

James Thurber wrote the satire *The Macbeth Murder Mystery*; in Willy Russell's play *Educating Rita* the protagonist is very enthusiastic about a performance of *Macbeth*, and Richard Willard Armour's *Twisted Tales from Shakespeare* are also "illustrated" by *Macbeth* cartoons.

Several lines of the play have become well-known quotations, e.g.:

> To-morrow, and to-morrow, and to-morrow
> Creeps in this petty pace from day to day
> To the last syllable of recorded time;
> And all our yesterdays have lighted fools
> The way to dusty death.
> (Act 5, Scene 5, lines 18–22)

This quotation was used by the South African president Mbeki in his State of the Nation Address on 3 February 2006 (cf. *www.info.gov.za/speeches/2006*) to emphasise that Macbeth's pessimism does not apply to the development in South Africa.

Shakespeare has even become a brand (cf. Farouky, 2006, pp. 48–53) and is used in advertising, sometimes in a totally inadequate way, e.g. by the former German cosmetics factory Mouson about 1970 for its soap products with Lady Macbeth's words: "All the perfumes of Arabia will not sweeten this little hand." (Act 5, Scene 1, lines 42–43)

Map of London Theatres c. 1600

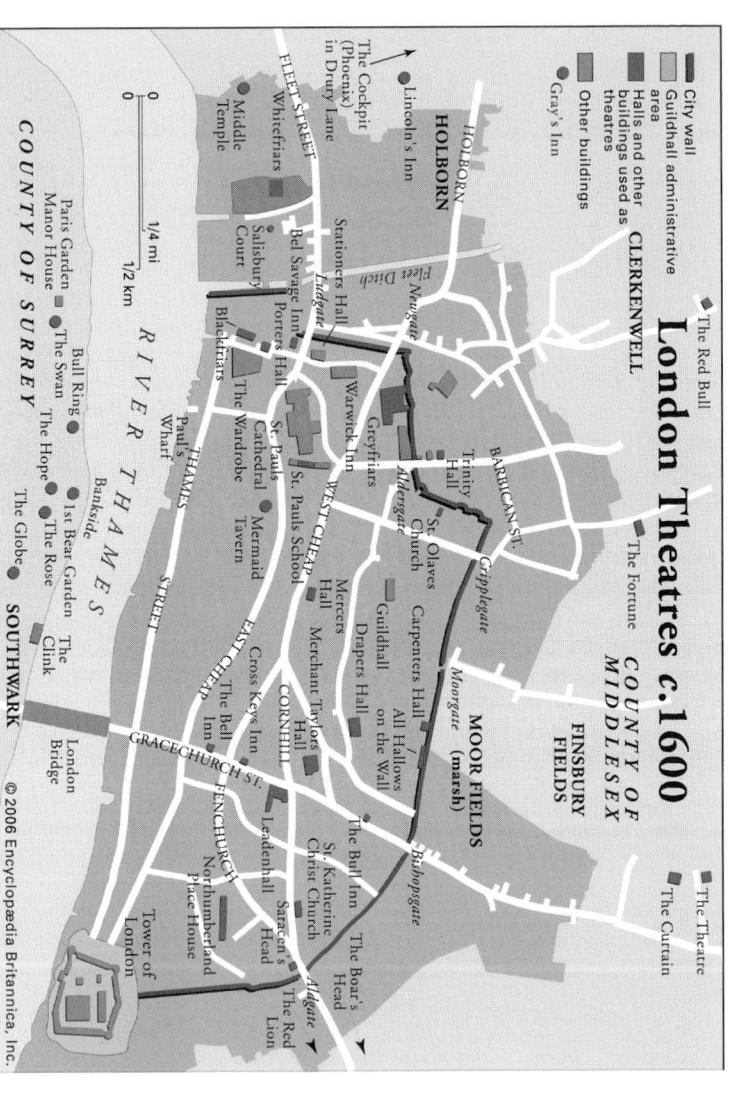

London Theatres c.1600

- City wall
- Guildhall administrative area
- Halls and other buildings used as theatres
- Other buildings

The Red Bull

The Cockpit (Phoenix) in Drury Lane

Lincoln's Inn

Gray's Inn

Middle Temple

Whitefriars

FLEET STREET

HOLBORN

CLERKENWELL

Fleet Ditch

Stationers' Hall

Bel Savage Inn

Ludgate

Salisbury Court

Porters Hall

Blackfriars

Paul's Wharf

Warwick Inn

Newgate

St. Paul's School

Mermaid Tavern

The Wardrobe

St. Paul's Cathedral

Greyfriars

WEST CHEAP

Aldersgate

Trinity Hall

BARBICAN ST.

Cripplegate

St. Olave's Church

Merchant Taylors Hall

Mercers Hall

Guildhall

Drapers Hall

Carpenters Hall

All Hallows on the Wall

Moorgate

MOOR FIELDS (marsh)

Bishopsgate

The Fortune

FINSBURY FIELDS

The Theatre

The Curtain

COUNTY OF MIDDLESEX

The Bull Inn

The Boar's Head

St. Katherine Christ Church

Aldgate

Saracen's Head

The Red Lion

Leadenhall

Northumberland Place House

FENCHURCH ST.

CORNHILL

The Bell Inn

Cross Keys Inn

EAST CHEAP

GRACECHURCH ST.

London Bridge

Tower of London

COUNTY OF SURREY

RIVER THAMES STREET

Bull Ring

Manor House

Paris Garden

The Swan

The Hope

1st Bear Garden

The Rose

The Globe

SOUTHWARK

Bankside

The Clink

0 1/4 mi
0 1/2 km

V   Impulses and Model Tasks

The following impulses and tasks are not intended to be dealt with exactly as they are offered here. You may, of course, adapt them more or less to your own ideas and alternatives of approach and analysis. They are structured according to the aspects of comprehension, analysis, comment, and creative writing. As Shakespeare and his works are also influenced by the political, economic, religious and cultural situation during the reigns of Elizabeth I and James I, you should also refer to Shakespeare's historical and biographical background.

1. Comprehension

1.1 Shakespeare's times

Write an essay about the main events during the reigns of Elizabeth I and James I.

- Elizabeth I, daughter of Henry VIII and Anne Boleyn, became Queen of England in 1558.
- Her rather strict reign is also called the Golden Age since peace and prosperity spread in England after the victory over the Spanish Armada in 1588 when England became a sea power.
- Queen Elizabeth was highly educated and promoted education and the arts.
- Many theatres were built in London to entertain the growing number of citizens who also enjoyed such cruel entertainment as bear-baiting and executions.
- Whereas Elizabeth's predecessor Queen Mary had tried to re-establish the Catholic creed in England and had persecuted Anglicans and Puritans, Queen Elizabeth demanded that Catholics and Puritans also had to attend the services of the Anglican Church.
- She was never married and declared that she was only married to England.
- Because of political rivalries, intrigues of the Court and plots to murder the Queen, her rule was also endangered. That is why she finally signed the death sentence against Mary Stuart of Scotland, whose guilt, however, had not been proved.
- After Elizabeth's death in 1603, Mary Stuart's son James VI of Scotland also became King of England as James I.
- James I was more interested in book-learning and witchcraft than in promoting the country as a sea power.
- He became the patron of Shakespeare's players' company The King's Men and thus also influenced Shakespeare to refer to the King in some scenes of *Macbeth*.
- He survived the Gunpowder Plot in 1605, which Shakespeare also alludes to in *Macbeth*.

1.2   Shakespeare's life

Make notes on the most important biographical facts for a talk in class.

- Baptised: April 26th, 1564 in Trinity Church, Stratford-upon-Avon; born probably three days before.
- Father: John Shakespeare married to Mary Arden, wealthy glover and tradesman, alderman and mayor.
- William probably attended Stratford grammar school, read classical Latin and Greek writers.
- His father's economic decline and end of political career.
- Shakespeare married Anne Hathaway in 1582, they had three children.
- Uncertain when he left for London where, according to the playwright Greene, he was in 1592 and already a successful playwright.
- In 1594 member of the players' company Lord Chamberlain's Men, under James I called The King's Men.
- Economically successful and able to buy the title of a gentleman for his father and himself in 1596 and some houses in Stratford a year later.
- In 1599 joint owner of The Globe Theatre.
- Probably left London to live in Stratford as a rich man in 1612.
- In 1616 he died in Stratford, probably on his birthday, buried in Trinity Church.

1.3   Shakespeare's works

Make a list of his main works according to the genres of the texts and explain them. Choose one of the plays and write down its plot. You can find help for instance in Louise McConnell's *Dictionary of Shakespeare* and in other books or on the Internet (cf. Bibliography on pp. 108 f).

- Genres of the plays according to the First Folio edition in 1623: histories, tragedies, comedies and romances.
- No clear dividing line between tragedies and histories, which could also be called tragedies due to the rise and fall of kings such as *Richard III*.
- Several of the best-known tragedies are read or performed at school, e.g. *Macbeth*, *Romeo and Juliet*, *Julius Caesar*, *Hamlet* and *King Lear*.
- The comedies mainly deal with love and friendship and after some funny and confusing events lead to a happy ending; some of them are also read or performed at school, e.g. *A Midsummer's Night's Dream* and *As You Like It*.
- Romances such as *The Tempest* can also be called tragicomedies.
- In the tragedies there can also be comic scenes, e.g. the porter scene in *Macbeth*.

- Shakespeare's *The Merchant of Venice* is called a comedy though the Jew's role is rather tragic.
- Shakespeare's poems and particularly his 154 sonnets are poetic master-pieces.

1.4 Shakespeare's theatre

Describe and explain the Shakespearean theatre, its players and audience by making use of a picture (see for instance p. 18).

- The theatre building: hexagonal or octagonal, three galleries inside and a stage protruding into the auditorium; no roof; on top of the rear building is a turret with a flag and a trumpeter to announce the beginning of the stage performance.
- The stage is not subdivided but different scenes could be performed at the front or rear of the stage; no curtain.
- At the rear there is the property-room for the costumes and stage property and above this is a gallery for spectators, which can also be used for scenes on a balcony or wall of a castle.
- The dressing-room is underneath the stage with a trapdoor, e.g. for the appearance and disappearance of the witches in *Macbeth*.
- Sounds such as the noise of battle-scenes, thunder and lightning are produced by fire-workers and fog by burning resin.
- Apart from the professional players there are walk-on parts; women's roles are played by boys.
- The audience from all social strata; the "groundlings" stand around the stage; the galleries are for the spectators of higher ranks who can also sit on stools on the stage.

1.5   Shakespeare's *Macbeth*

Outline the plot of the play. Only mention the most important events.

Act 1
- The witches' spell as the leitmotif of the play
- Macbeth's victory over the rebels against King Duncan
- The witches' predictions about Macbeth's and Banquo's futures
- Macbeth's ambition and moral conflict
- Lady Macbeth's influence on her husband

Act 2
- Duncan's murder and Macbeth's remorse
- Discovery of the murder and the escape of Duncan's sons
- Macbeth, the new King

Act 3
- Macbeth's fear and Banquo's murder
- The appearance of Banquo's Ghost at Macbeth's banquet and Macbeth's and his wife's reactions
- Macbeth as a tyrant

Act 4
- The prophecies of the apparitions and Macbeth's false sense of security
- The murder of Macduff's family
- Macduff's and Malcolm's determination to fight Macbeth

Act 5
- Lady Macbeth sleepwalking, haunted by the remembrance of Duncan's murder
- The approach of the English army and Macbeth being troubled by revolts and desertions
- According to the apparitions' prophecies, he feels invulnerable and continues fighting though one prediction after the other turns out to be a deceit
- Lady Macbeth's suicide, Macbeth killed by Macduff and Malcolm as the new King

2. Analysis and Interpretation

2.1 Describe and explain Macbeth's development from a brave and loyal subject of King Duncan to his murderer.

- Macbeth's courage and loyalty
- His ambition to become king
- The ambiguous predictions of the witches and Macbeth's reaction
- Lady Macbeth's determination to make her husband king, and her influence on him
- Macbeth's moral doubts
- His hallucination of a dagger and decision to murder the King
- Macbeth's horror and remorse

2.2 Analyse the witches' role in the play and their impact on the audience.

a) **Their role in the play**
- The witches' mingling good and evil as the keynote of the play.
- Their so-called prophecies are meant to delude Macbeth since they first just mention Macbeth's position as Thane of Glamis, then tell him that he will become Thane of Cawdor, which has already been decided by Duncan, and finally influence him to become king.
- They also seem to influence Lady Macbeth when she calls upon the evil spirits to make her cruel and relentless.
- As Macbeth still fears to be endangered after Banquo's murder, he wants to know his fate and is again cheated by the witches' apparitions.
- His false sense of security leads to his death.

b) **Their impact on the audience**
- Shakespeare makes use of witches in his play to please his patron James I, who wrote a book about witchcraft and also saw the play.
- As the belief in witchcraft was common in his times, Shakespeare makes the play more interesting and fascinating to his audience.
- The conflict between good and evil is presented as the confrontation of God's order and the devil's chaos which is both mirrored in nature, society and man's moral conflict.
- The audience is challenged to reflect on this conflict or admonished to resist the evil and acknowledge God's order, which implies obeying the rightful king as the representative of God on earth.

2.3 Describe the relationship between Macbeth and his wife.

- They are ambitious and want to become king and queen.
- Lady Macbeth is determined to do everything to support her husband to become king.
- At the beginning of the play Lady Macbeth seems to be "stronger" than Macbeth because she successfully urges him to become a murderer.
- They seem to love each other since Macbeth's first words to her after his return home are: "My dearest love" (Act 1, Scene 5, line 56). But Lady Macbeth can only love him if he behaves as a "man", who is without fear and moral doubts: "From this time, / Such I account thy love. Art thou afeard / To be the same in thine own act and valour, / As thou art in desire?" (Act 1, Scene 7, lines 38–41)
- Lady Macbeth plans the murder, supports her husband and helps him by feigning their innocence and also by trying to deceive the lords at the banquet when Macbeth is horrified by Banquo's Ghost.
- But in the middle of the play Macbeth does not inform her about his plan to murder Banquo, whereas his wife asks him for the first time: "What's to be done?" (Act 3, Scene 2, line 44). Macbeth's answer is: "Be innocent of the knowledge, dearest chuck, / Till thou applaud the deed" (lines 45–46). Their roles change now since Lady Macbeth has become rather passive whereas Macbeth begins to play the active part until the end of the play.
- Macbeth tells his wife that he wants to ask the witches about his future, but after that Lady Macbeth disappears from the stage until in Act 5, when she appears for the last time as a helpless and mentally sick sleep-walker who is tortured by her guilty conscience.
- Though the doctor admits that he cannot cure his wife, Macbeth asks him to try.
- When Macbeth is informed of his wife's death, he does not seem to be deeply moved by it but only broods on the absurdity of life.

2.4 Describe and analyse the differences between a good and a bad king as presented in this play by also comparing Macbeth with Duncan and Malcolm.

a) Traits of a bad and sinful king
- Though Macbeth is troubled by moral doubts at the beginning of the play, he commits a regicide and thus violates God's order and develops into a bloodthirsty tyrant who also hires murderers to kill his friend Banquo and Macduff's family. At the end of the play he seems to be the personification of evil and is called a devil.

- Macbeth is a courageous soldier but too weak to resist the evil influences of the witches and his wife.
- Before his death, Macbeth despairingly describes himself as without "honour, love, obedience, troops of friends" (Act 5, Scene 3, line 25) but cursed and hated by everybody.
- Shakespeare describes the main characteristics of a bad king when Malcolm enumerates the vices of Macbeth: "I grant him bloody [murderous], / Luxurious [lecherous], avaricious [greedy], false, deceitful, / Sudden [violent], malicious, smacking of every sin / That has a name" (Act 4, Scene 3, lines 57–60). Thus Shakespeare refers to the seven deadly sins in Christian religion since the Early Fathers that result in damnation: *superbia* (pride), *avaritia* (greed), *gastrimargia* (gluttony), *fornicatio* or *luxuria* (voluptuousness), *accidia* (sloth), *invidia* (envy), and *ira* (rage).

b) Traits of a good or even ideal king

- Whereas King Duncan is a gracious and just but guileless king, his son Malcolm is also cautious and sceptical after his father's death and when he meets Macduff, who could be Macbeth's spy. When he tells Macduff that he would be a voluptious and avaricious king, Macduff plays those vices down as acceptable for a king, which seems to hint at the fact that a king need not be ideal but should strive to be a good king.
- Malcolm lists twelve virtues a good king should have: "justice, verity [truthfulness], temp'rance [moderation], stableness [firmness], bounty [generosity], perseverance [endurance], mercy [forgiveness], low-liness [humility], devotion [piety], patience, courage, fortitude [strength, constancy]" (Act 4, Scene 3, lines 92–94).
- Shakespeare characterises the English King Edward the Confessor as an ideal king when he emphasises his holiness, his ability to cure people miraculously, and his "heavenly gift of prophecy" (Act 4, Scene 3, line 159).
- King Edward helps Malcolm and Macduff by sending troops against Macbeth to liberate Scotland from tyranny and establish God's order again.
- Possibly Shakespeare also wanted to remind his patron James I of the qualities a king should possess.

2.5 Analyse how Shakespeare creates and maintains interior suspense by giving some examples.

- The witches spell "Fair is foul, and foul is fair" as the keynote of the play
- Macbeth's and Banquo's reaction to the witches' predictions

- Macbeth's ambition to become king and his secret wish to murder Duncan
- Lady Macbeth's determination to urge Macbeth to murder Duncan
- Macbeth's moral conflict (cf. his soliloquy at the beginning of Act 1, Scene 7), his hallucination of a dagger and his final decision (cf. his soliloquy at the end of Act 2, Scene 1)
- Lady Macbeth's excitement and her husband's horror during and after the deed, also expressed by stichomythia (cf. Act 2, Scene 2, lines 16 ff)
- Their deceitful behaviour and pretended alibi (cf. Act 2, Scene 3)
- Macbeth's fear of Banquo and his decision to challenge fate (cf. Act 3, Scene 1)
- His horror of Banquo's Ghost and his revealing reaction (cf. Act 3, Scene 4)
- The apparitions' prophecies and his false sense of security (cf. Act 4, Scene 1)
- His going on fighting and realisation of having been cheated by the apparitions' prophecies one after the other

2.6 Describe and analyse Shakespeare's use of dramatic irony. Give some examples referring to different characters of the play.

- Shakespeare frequently employs dramatic irony in his play to emphasise the discrepancy between what seems to be true and what is really true.
- For instance Shakespeare introduces Macbeth by nearly the same words as the witches. Though Macbeth is not aware of it and refers to the bad weather (*foul*) and his victory (*fair*), he is already characterised as being under the evil influence of the witches.
- Though Duncan knows that it is impossible to read man's thoughts in his face (cf. Act 1, Scene 4, lines 11 ff) and was betrayed by Cawdor, he absolutely trusts Macbeth: "we love him highly" (Act 1, Scene 6, line 30).
- Banquo mentions a bird that has built its nest in the wall of Macbeth's castle because it feels safe there (cf. Act 1, Scene 6, lines 7–8) when he approaches the castle with Duncan, who in no way feels endangered as Macbeth's guest, though his host becomes his murderer.
- Lady Macbeth asks her husband when Duncan will leave again and gets the answer: "Tomorrow, as he purposes" (Act 1, Scene 5, line 58).
- Lady Macbeth admonishes her husband not to think so "brain-sickly" of Duncan's murder (cf. Act 2, Scene 2, line 49) or it will make them mad and believes that "a little water clears us of this deed" (line 70). At the end of the play she really is mad and tries to wash the imagined blood from her hands in vain.
- At his banquet, Macbeth wishes that Banquo were present without seeing that Banquo's Ghost has already entered.

2.7   Analyse how Duncan's murder is mirrored in nature.

- While Macbeth is murdering Duncan, his wife hears the hooting of an owl, which was believed to be an omen of death. She calls the bird "the fatal bellman", referring to a man ringing a bell when a coffin was carried through the streets (cf. Act 2, Scene 2, line 3).
- Lennox describes the night of Duncan's murder as chaotic: violent storm, cries of grief, screams of death, the permanent hooting of the owl, earthquake (cf. Act 2, Scene 3, lines 46 ff).
- An old man tells Ross that he has never experienced such a horrible night, which according to Ross does not end though it is already daytime. They mention the unnatural behaviour of an owl and Duncan's horses that even ate each other (cf. Act 2, Scene 4).

2.8   Describe and analyse the list of characters and the formal and structural elements of the play.

a) List of characters
- One protagonist: Macbeth
- Some major characters: the three witches, Lady Macbeth, Banquo, Malcolm, Macduff and Duncan
- Several minor characters such as Donaldbain, the Captain, Fleance, Ross, Lennox, Lady Macduff and her son, the Genlewoman and the Doctor, Siward and his son
- Walk-on parts of lords, soldiers, servants and messengers
- As the play is mainly set in Scotland, the majority of the characters are Scottish: King Duncan and his sons, the Scottish thanes, the members of their households and their supporters. Only three characters are English: Siward and his son, a doctor. The third group of characters represents the supernatural sphere of evil powers: three witches and apparitions, Hecate and her three witches.

b) Formal elements
- Five acts subdivided into a different number of scenes
- Different places in Scotland, one scene at the English Court and different times mostly at night
- Dialogues and soliloquies written in blank verse (iambic pentameter without a rhyme)
- Sometimes a rhyming couplet signals the end of an act or scene to the audience.
- Some important statements e.g. of Lady Macbeth are emphasised by a rhyme (cf. Act 3, Scene 2, lines 4 ff).

- The witches use tetrameter (lines of four stressed syllables) and pair-rhyme, which stresses the difference from the human world, i.e. their supernatural powers and their magic activities.
- To make the dialogue more dynamic according to the action, Shakespeare also uses enjambement and subdivides the lines in different parts spoken by different characters.
- To intensify the interior tension of a dialogue, Shakespeare sometimes uses stichomythia, for example in Act 2, Scene 2, lines 16 ff when after Duncan's murder Macbeth and his wife are extremely excited and horrified and exchange very short or even one-word sentences.
- Shakespeare also employs prose sometimes, e.g. when Lady Macbeth reads her husband's letter (cf. Act 1, Scene 5, lines 1 ff). Also Macbeth uses prose when he reminds the hired murderers of Banquo of his (false) accusations against his friend (cf. Act 3, Scene 1). Lady Macbeth and her husband welcome their guests in prose at the beginning of the Banquet Scene (Act 3, Scene 4). The porter speaks his rude text in prose and is thus also characterised as belonging to an inferior social class (cf. Act 2, Scene 3). Prose is also used to underline the childlike talk of Lady Macduff and her son (cf. Act 4, Scene 2), and Lady Macbeth's sleepwalking and madness (Act 5, Scene 1).

c) The structure of the play
- Act 1: exposition, i.e. introduction to the place, time and main action of the play; indirect characterisation of Macbeth
- Act 2: rising action, i.e. the witches' predictions, Macbeth's moral conflict, Lady Macbeth's evil influence on her husband, Duncan's murder and the escape of his sons
- Act 3: climax and turning point; Macbeth's horror on seeing Banquo's Ghost, the lords' suspicion and the tyrant's decision to kill everybody who stands in his way
- Act 4: falling action; the apparitions' ambiguous prophecies and Macbeth's false sense of security, preparations of a "holy war" against the tyrant at the English Court
- Act 5: denouement; the final battle, Lady Macbeth's and her husband's deaths and the restoration of order by the new King

2.9 Analyse Shakespeare's use of stylistic devices and their effects.

Shakespeare uses several stylistic devices and frequently combines them to make the characters' speech more graphic and to emphasise their ideas and feelings.

Thus he employs a lot of images, metaphors, comparisons, symbols and allegories or personifications to convey a vivid impression to his audience and enable them to imagine things and be impressed by the mainly sinister atmosphere and cruel events.

Shakespeare frequently uses antithesis, paradox, alliteration, repetition, enumeration and parallelism for emphasis.

a) Shakespeare's imagery and other stylistic devices that make his language more graphic

- Most of the images used by Shakespeare refer to nature, night and blood, e.g. nature's apocalyptic destruction during the night of Duncan's murder (cf. Act 2, Scene 3, lines 46 ff) or Macbeth's wading in a river of blood (cf. Act 3, Scene 4, lines 136 ff).
- Frequently Shakespeare employs metaphors referring to nature and man, e.g. "full of scorpions is my mind" (Act 3, Scene 2, line 36), also combined with images, e.g. when Macbeth's fear of Banquo is described as a venomous and dangerous snake (cf. Act 3, Scene 2, lines 13 ff). Metaphors are e.g. used when Banquo's descendants are called "seeds" and "chickens" replaces children, the sun becomes "the travelling lamp" and "crown" is used instead of head. For life, the metaphors of a walking shadow, a poor player and a meaningless tale are used (cf. Act 5, Scene 5, lines 23 ff).
- Man is compared to several animals that symbolise various virtues, e.g. eagles, lions and bears that symbolise courage; cowards are compared to fearful animals such as sparrows and hares. Night-birds or black birds such as owls and ravens symbolise death.
- The loud knocking at the castle's gate at night symbolises the knocking of death on man's door or his pricks of conscience.
- Shakespeare also uses allegories such as Fortune (Act 1, Scene 2, line 17; Act 5, Scene 7, line 23), Fate (Act 3, Scene 1, line 72) and justice (Act 1, Scene 7, line 10: "This even-handed justice") and personifies for instance night (Act 1, Scene 5, lines 48 ff: "Come, thick night [...]") and sleep (cf. Act 2, Scene 2, lines 39 ff).

b) Shakespeare's stylistic devices used for emphasis

- Shakespeare frequently employs several stylistic devices such as alliteration and repetition for emphasis, e.g. "beard to beard" and "beat them backward" (Act 5, Scene 5, lines 6–7) to stress Macbeth's determination to fight and his false sense of security, or "Bleed, bleed, poor country" (Act 4, Scene 3, line 31) to stress Macduff's despair.
- He enumerates the vices of a tyrant and the virtues of an ideal king to make the audience and probably also King James I aware of the differences (cf. Act 4, Scene 3, lines 57 ff; 91 ff).

- The conflict between good and evil is underlined by antithesis, frequently additionally stressed by other stylistic devices such as alliteration, repetition and parallel sentences as in Macbeth's soliloquy after the witches' predictions in the first act of the play.
  Already at the beginning of the play the strong influence of the witches' spell on the action of the play is underscored by a paradoxical antithesis and alliteration but particularly by its structure, since the mixing of good and evil is presented by chiasm. Also the apparitions' prophecies in Act 4 sound paradoxical.
- To intensify the impact of Macbeth's words at the end of the play Shakespeare combines numerous poetic devices that contribute to the graphic nature of the speech and convey Macbeth's nihilistic view of life, such as metaphors, images, personification and assonance. He combines them with stylistic means that stress the protagonist's weary mood such as repetition, alliteration, parallelism and enumeration (cf. e.g. Act 5, Scene 5, lines 18 ff).

2.10 Analyse a part of the play or deal with a topic you find most interesting and give reasons why. You could also recite or perform a soliloquy or scene of the play.

It should not be ignored that Shakespeare did not write *Macbeth* to be read, but to be performed on a stage. That is why you should not only imagine its performance when reading the text but also reflect on how parts of the play or even the whole drama could be performed on stage. In the Cambridge School Shakespeare edition of *Macbeth* (edited by Rex Gibson, Cambridge: Cambridge University Press, 2005) you can find numerous suggestions and examples of adapting the written text to its performance.

- "Fair is foul, and foul is fair" as the leitmotif of the play
- Macbeth's development as mirrored in his soliloquies
- Lady Macbeth's self-characterisation in her soliloquies and the sleep-walking scene
- Chaos and order in *Macbeth* and its impact on the audience
- The play's circular structure: rebellion against Duncan – restoration of order – Duncan's murder and Macbeth's tyranny – war against Macbeth and the restoration of order by Malcolm
- References to the Elizabethan world and James I
- My favourite soliloquy

3.   Comments

If you like to give your opinion about the play or parts of it based on arguments, here are some suggestions:

- Arguments for and/or against the omission of the Hecate scene (Act 3, Scene 5) and her appearance in Act 4, Scene 1, lines 39–43.
- Some ideas *pro*: The Hecate scene was not written by Shakespeare but by his contemporary, the playwright Thomas Middleton; the scene does not really promote the action, it does not contribute to a better understanding of the play or of Macbeth's conflict and ruin; the image of "elves and fairies" is not fitting in this scene about witches.
- Some ideas *contra*: Hecate is also mentioned by Macbeth in his soliloquy (Act 2, Scene 1, line 52) and before Banquo's murder in Act 3, Scene 2, line 41; Hecate is the mistress of the witches they have to obey; the audience gets to know that there is a hierarchy of evil powers; James I might have enjoyed the Hecate scene and her music and dance in Act 4, Scene 1.
- "Faults" of the play or unnecessary subplots, e.g. the disappearance of Donaldbain and Fleance.
- Comment on Shakespeare's decision not to show Duncan's and Lady Macduff's murder on stage but confront the audience with the murder of Macbeth's friend Banquo and of a child (Macduff's son).
- Comment on the social role of men and women and the presentation of children (Fleance and Macduff's son) in *Macbeth*.
- Comment on a professional review of a stage performance of *Macbeth* or its filmic adaptation. (You can also find reviews on the Internet.)
- Write a review of a performance of *Macbeth* you saw in the theatre or as a movie.
- Shakespeare finishes *Macbeth* with the restoration of order whereas at the end of Polanski's film Duncan's son Donaldbain appears again to visit the witches, which alludes to the continuation of violence and murder. Write a comment.
- The famous British actor Sir Laurence Olivier said, "Macbeth shows how to stop overreaching ambition from derailing you." Comment on this statement.
- The stage-director Günther Rennert explained his production of *Macbeth* at the Burgtheater in Vienna by saying: "Macbeth is dead but the evil remains." Write a comment.
- The Polish critic Jan Kott (*Shakespeare Our Contemporary*, 1964) believes that Shakespeare's *Macbeth* and his other tragedies and histories anticipated the tyranny of Hitler and Stalin. Comment on this statement.

- The relevance of Shakespeare's *Macbeth* today (after 400 years): Is *Macbeth* giving you a deeper insight into yourself, the people around you or the present political and social situation? Some aspects: ambition – modesty, justice – injustice, order – tyranny/chaos, moral conflict between good and evil, love – hatred, friendship – betrayal/isolation, truth – lie, peace – war, belief – superstition, courage – fear, hope – despair, meaningful life – absurdity/nihilism
- The topic of the Shakespeare-Tage of the German Shakespeare-Gesellschaft in Weimar from 20–23 April, 2006 was: "Violence and Terror" in Shakespeare's works and their performances. At a panel discussion, the question was raised to what extent "staging violence and terror" contributes to the understanding of the plays. Write a comment.

4. Writing Essays or Term Papers about *Macbeth* Adaptations

After studying and analysing Shakespeare's *Macbeth*, you might wish to analyse, compare and comment on a film production or other adaptations of the play, e.g. by writing a review.

- Orson Welles' black-and-white film *Macbeth* (1947) – a film review.
- Roman Polanski's film *Macbeth* (1971) – a film review. Mind Polanski's changes to the play, in particular the visualisation of extreme violence and the different ending.
- Compare the advantages and disadvantages of Orson Welles' and Polanski's *Macbeth* adaptation.
- Jack Gold's *Macbeth* (BBC) (1983) – a film review.
- Compare the cinematic presentation of Macbeth and his wife in different films.
- Compare stills of the same character taken from different films.
- Write a filmscript of a scene you would like to perform.
- Giuseppe Verdi's opera *Macbeth* (1865).
- James Thurber's satire *The Macbeth Murder Mystery*.
- Rita's reaction to a performance of *Macbeth* in Willy Russell's play *Educating Rita*.
- Analyse the film *Elizabeth* (1998) and compare it with the presentation of Queen Elizabeth I in a history book.
- The reconstructed Globe Theatre opened in London near its original site in Southwark in 1996. There are also newly built Globe theatres e.g. in Neuss and Tokyo. Write an essay based on the information you can get from the theatres and on the Internet.

Some of the following aspects could be considered when you analyse a stage production, a film, etc and compare it to Shakespeare's play.

- Techniques of adaptation: reduction of the whole play or part of it; expansion of the play by additional dialogues, scenes, etc; transformation of the play into a film, opera, narrative text, satire, etc
- Elements of a traditional or modernising presentation referring to place, time, characters, clothes, stage equipment, sound effects, etc
- Cinematic elements such as location, time, actors, camera work, film colour / black-and-white, lighting, musical score, sound effects, etc
- Satirical elements: exaggeration, irony, criticism
- The impact of a performance of *Macbeth* on a spectator such as Rita in Russell's play

- Verdi's setting of Shakespeare's *Macbeth*: number of acts and scenes, place and time, the development of the action, costumes, lighting, musical instruments, singers, chorus, ballet, etc
- Comparison of a performance of *Macbeth* at the new Globe Theatre to the performance at a modern theatre

At the end of your essay you could also give your view and evaluation of the stage production, the film or text.

The topics mentioned above could also inspire you to write a term paper ('Facharbeit') about one of these or other themes you find worth working on. Information about the themes can be found in libraries or on the Internet (cf. the Bibliography).

Bibliography

Armour, Richard William: Twisted Tales from Shakespeare. New York: Mc-Graw-Hill, 1957.

Bradley, A. C.: Shakespearean Tragedy. London: Macmillan, 1962.

Browning, Peter / Arndt, Reinhold: Some Data About Shakespeare. In: William Shakespeare: Macbeth. Revised Edition. Ed. by A. Leonhardi. Dortmund: Lensing.

Dale, F. Coye: Pronouncing Shakespeare's Words. A Guide from A to Zounds. Westport (Conn.): Greenwood Press, 1998.

Dale, Vera K. G.: Shakespeare and the Age that Made Him. Stuttgart/Düsseldorf/Berlin/Leipzig: Ernst Klett Verlag, 2003.

Dutton, Richard / Howard, Jean E.: A Companion to Shakespeare's Works. Vol. 1: The Tragedies. Malden: Blackwell, 2003.

Farouky, Jumana: Shakespeare Inc. In: TIME, March 27, 2006, pp. 48–53.

Hall, Peter: There Is No Final Shakespeare. Life, Language, Literature. Stuttgart: Klett, 1985, pp. 234f.

McConnell, Louise: Dictionary of Shakespeare. Teddington: Peter Collin, 2000.

Paris, Jean: William Shakespeare in Selbstzeugnissen und Dokumenten. Reinbek bei Hamburg: Rowohlt, 1958.

Poppe, Reiner: William Shakespeare. Stuttgart: Reclam, 2000. (Literaturwissen für Schule und Studium.)

Posener, Alan: William Shakespeare. Reinbek bei Hamburg: Rowohlt, 1999.

Rothwell, Kenneth S.: A History of Shakespeare on Screen. A Century of Film and Television. Second Edition. Cambridge: Cambridge University Press, 2004.

Schabert, Ina (Ed.): Shakespeare-Handbuch. Fourth Edition. Stuttgart: Alfred Kröner, 2000.

Schoenbaum, Samuel: William Shakespeare. A Documentary Life. Oxford: The Clarendon Press, 1975.

Shakespeare, William: Macbeth. Ed. by Rex Gibson. Cambridge: Cambridge University Press, 2005.

Shakespeare's Holinshed. The Chronicle and the Historical Plays Compared by W. G. Boswell-Stone. London: Lawrence and Bullen, 1896.

Shakespeare, William: Macbeth. Directed by Roman Polanski. Columbia Pictures 1971 (DVD).

Scott, Robert Owen: William Shakespeare, *Macbeth*. Fourteenth Edition. Stuttgart: Klett, 2005. (Barron's Book Notes.)

Suerbaum, Ulrich: Das elisabethanische Zeitalter. Stuttgart: Reclam, 1989.

– Der Shakespeare-Führer. Stuttgart: Reclam, 2001. Revised Edition 2006.

Thurber, James: The Macbeth Murder Mystery. In: The Thurber Carnival. Harmondsworth: Penguin, 1979, pp. 83–86.

Tillyard, E. M. W.: The Elizabethan World Picture. Harmondsworth: Penguin, 1963.

Trevelyan, George Macaulay: A Shortened History of England. Harmondsworth: Penguin, 1960.

– Shakespeare's England. Selected Chapters from English Social History. Ed. by B. Greive. Bielefeld/Berlin/Hannover: Velhagen & Klasing.

The following websites are also useful:

Shakespeare Resource Centre: www.bardweb.net
Shakespeare's Macbeth: http://en.wikipedia.org/wiki/Macbeth
Shakespeare's theatre performances: www.onlineshakespeare.com
Shakespearean Glossary: http://eserver.org/langs/shakespeare-glossary.txt
Shakespeare's Tragedies on Film: www.jetlink.net
Shakespeare's Globe: www.shakespeare-globe.org.uk
Reviews: http://mrshowbiz.go.com, www.imdb

Acknowledgements

S. 7 und S. 18: Picture-Alliance, Frankfurt/M. / KPA/HIP – S. 10: Picture-Alliance, Frankfurt/M. / AKG – S. 13: Corbis, Düsseldorf / Morris – S. 16: Corbis, Düsseldorf / Historical Picture Archive – S. 83: Corbis, Düsseldorf / Pawel Libera – S. 86: Cinetext, Frankfurt/M. – S. 88: defd, Hamburg / Kinoarchiv – S. 90: Reprinted with permission from Encyclopaedia Britannica, © 1997 by Encyclopaedia Britannica, Inc.

Der Verlag hat sich nach bestem Wissen und Gewissen bemüht, alle Inhaber von Urheberrechten an Abbildungen zu diesem Werk ausfindig zu machen. Sollte das in irgendeinem Fall nicht korrekt geschehen sein, bitten wir um Entschuldigung und bieten an, gegebenenfalls in einer nachfolgenden Auflage einen korrigierten Quellennachweis zu bringen.

Die besten Karten im Abi

Die ersten Lernkarten fürs Abitur mit den 100 wichtigsten Aufgaben, die man im Abitur beherrschen muss. Die Karteikarten im A6-Format beinhalten Aufgaben, Lösungen und, auf der aufklappbaren Innenseite, ausführliches Wissen zum jeweiligen Thema.

ADDITIONAL INFORMATION 3

English | Facts about the UK and the USA | The British Prime Minister

In theory, the British prime minister is just a "primus inter pares" (the first among equals) and much of the prime minister's actual power depends on his/her strength and his/her authority as a party leader: As long as he/she enjoys the support of parliament, he/she can decisively shape the nation's policy.
Dominant prime ministers such as Margaret Thatcher and Tony Blair imposed strict party discipline, forcing the members of their parties to invariably support the government's policies and proposals if they did not want to be excluded. Thus Tony Blair became the most successful Labour prime minister.
For the prime minister it is essential not to lose the support of parliament. When Tony Blair came under increasing pressure from Labour MPs, he announced his resignation.

No. 10 Downing Street, the residence of the British prime minister
© Getty Images, München / Tim Graham

Abi-Lernbox Englisch
100 Lernkarten mit den wichtigsten Aufgaben und Lösungen
ISBN 978-3-12-929971-5 | 19,95 Euro

Lektürehilfen – Literatur verstehen

Lektürehilfen sind der Schlüssel zum besseren Verständnis von Literatur:

– Die wichtigen Themen kennen dank thematischer Kapitel.

– Die richtigen Antworten wissen durch die Vorbereitung mit typischen Abiturfragen.

– Inhaltsangabe der Lektüre als mp3-Download unter: www.klett.de/lernhilfen

Paul Auster
Moon Palace
ISBN 978-3-12-923046-6 | 9,95 €

T. C. Boyle
Tortilla Curtain
ISBN 978-3-12-923001-5 | 9,95 €

Arthur Miller
Death of a Salesman
ISBN 978-3-12-923048-0 | 9,95 €

Ray Bradbury
Fahrenheit 451
ISBN 978-3-12-923050-3 | 9,95 €

Willy Russell
Educating Rita
ISBN 978-3-12-923028-2 | 9,95 €

Caught between Cultures
ISBN 978-3-12-923016-9 | 9,95 €

William Shakespeare
Romeo and Juliet
ISBN 978-3-12-923039-8 | 9,95 €

Don DeLillo
Falling Man
ISBN 978-3-12-923053-4 | 9,95 €

Macbeth
ISBN 978-3-12-923038-1 | 9,95 €

Nick Hornby
About a Boy
ISBN 978-3-12-923003-9 | 9,95 €

Tennessee Williams
A Streetcar Named Desire
ISBN 978-3-12-923045-9 | 9,95 €